THE UNIVERSITY OF MICHIGAN
CENTER FOR CHINESE STUDIES

MICHIGAN PAPERS IN CHINESE STUDIES
NO. 21

REBELLION IN
NINETEENTH-CENTURY CHINA

by

Albert Feuerwerker

Ann Arbor

Center for Chinese Studies
The University of Michigan

1975

CONTENTS

PREFACE

This essay on the phenomenon of rebellion in nineteenth-century China is part of a larger work in progress which attempts an interpretation of the main events and trends of China's modern history. I would welcome comment and criticism of my sometimes idiosyncratic formulations. The reader will quickly note my especial indebtedness to my friend Philip A. Kuhn's truly important <u>Rebellion and Its Enemies in Late Imperial China: Militarization and Social Structure, 1796-1864</u> (Cambridge: Harvard University Press, 1970).

Albert Feuerwerker
Ann Arbor, Michigan
May 1975

INTRODUCTION

Nei-luan wai-huan, "domestic disorder and foreign calamities":
this is the formula with which countless textbooks for Chinese students
have summed up their country's fate in the century after the Opium
War. In this essay on "domestic disorder" I shall consider the
sources of social dissidence in late-Ch'ing China; the varieties (in
scale, ideology, and organization) of domestic rebellion; the range
of responses by state and society to these uprisings; and the consequences of rebellion and its suppression for a dynasty already shaken
by foreign invasion. My intention is to describe and analyze as one
broad social phenomenon--appearing and reappearing over the century
stretching from the White Lotus rebellion of 1796-1804 to the first
advent of uprisings of a new kind, symbolized by Sun Yat-sen's abortive revolt in Canton in 1895 and that of T'ang Ts'ai-chang in 1900--
a remarkable number and variety of unsuccessful challenges to the
Manchu regime. Of course, each of these events was local and
specific and occupied a particular chronological niche. At the same
time each reflected the underlying dynamics of nineteenth-century
Chinese society, both its singular stability and the contradictions
which could tear it asunder.

Popular rebellion in China, as is true elsewhere, was usually
the undertaking of the mostly illiterate lower classes, sometimes
inspired or assisted by a handful of disaffected intellectuals. The
written record of these events and those who participated in them is,
on the other hand, overwhelmingly the product of literate men of
power and wealth who suppressed these challenges to their authority
and status. With the altogether remarkable exception of the Taipings,
very few documents of rebel provenance were composed, or have survived if they were written. Nor has an attenuated oral tradition
yielded more than embellishments on the official record. These are
lacunae of some consequence. For great numbers of China's people--
from the millions who were swept up in such floodtides as the Taiping
uprising to the countless local eddies of protest against landlords and
wicked officials--these acts of insurrection were central facts in their
lives. The events, their leaders, the heightened expectations, even
the bitterness of defeat--these were of greater importance to them
than the posturings of emperors and officials, the disputations of
scholars, and even more important than the pretensions and impor-

1

tunities of the recently arrived "big nosed barbarians." But sadly
there is little that the historian can legitimately say about the motives
and attitudes--even about the identities--of the nameless masses who
sometimes rebelled against poverty and oppression. The story is in-
complete, possibly too neat and abstract--I caution the reader.

The rebellions which we are considering have been characterized
by historians in the People's Republic of China as peasant uprisings
(nung-min ch'i-i, literally, "righteous uprisings of the peasantry").
In his essay on "The Chinese Revolution and the Chinese Communist
Party" (1940), which has become the locus classicus for the interpretation of China's modern history in the P.R.C., Mao Tse-tung asserted that prior to the twentieth century, because of their great
number and gigantic scale, "these peasant uprisings and peasant wars
alone formed the real motive force in China's historical evolution."
However, he continued, without "the leadership of an advanced class
and an advanced political party, such as the correct leadership given
by the proletariat and the Communist Party today, the peasant revolutions invariably failed." Having rejected the court-centered "feudal"
history composed by the traditional elite (whose domination of Chinese
society was shattered by the CCP victory over the Kuomintang), Communist historiography turned to these peasant uprisings in an attempt
to construct a new, popular, and progressive past. The central the-
sis of the new history may be briefly summarized: Although ignored
or despised by the intellectuals of the old ruling class, who saw them
only as disorders (luan) and told exclusively the story of emperors
and officials, the class struggles of the popular masses--most of whom
were peasants--had on repeated occasions pushed the contradictions of
"feudal" society to their limits and thereby in some measure stimulate
the development of premodern Chinese civilization.

While their writings apply Mao's dictum about the ideological and
political limitations of peasant rebellion, P.R.C. historians have, par
adoxically but perhaps understandably, in at least two respects fallen
into the expository mode of the "feudal" officials and intellectuals who
despatches and letters provide us with most of what we now can know
of these movements. First, like the Ch'ing generals who exaggerated
the size and cohesiveness of the White Lotus or Nien armed bands--
in order to cover up their own incapacities or to justify continued ex-
penditure of imperial funds from which they "squeezed" their shares--
the recent historiography to which I refer tends not be overly precise
about the organizational coherence and ideological clarity, that is, the

degree of institutionalization, of these movements. Indeed, perhaps a hundred uprisings of more than petty local scope can be identified in the Ch'ing period. But they took place within a "hierarchy of dissidence," as I shall call it, which requires that we distinguish at least the following: 1) spontaneous, usually small-scale and local antiofficial or antilandlord actions; 2) interlineage and communal "feuds"; 3) the religious and secular "underworld"; 4) banditry; 5) rebellion; and 6) revolution. I shall discuss this hierarchy at greater length below. Unavoidably, in the discussion that follows, I shall repeatedly use "rebellion" or "insurrection" as nontechnical, generic terms for these social movements. The context should make clear what I intend.

Second, an analysis of popular uprisings which limits itself to asserting the "peasant" composition of these movements, with the occasional admission that leaders may come from other classes so long as they "served the peasant class," impedes a comprehension of the dynamics of nineteenth-century Chinese society as much as the Ch'ing officials' attempt to squeeze these phenomena all into the same box of heterodox sectarianism. Both peasants and secret societies, of course, were essential ingredients of the anti-Ch'ing popular movements. But to ignore, in particular, the ambigous relationship of popular social dissidence to the "orthodox" and "elite" components of Chinese society impoverishes any explanation of their origin, course, and consequences.

THE REBELLIONS

The largely narrative account of rebellion in this section will be followed by a more systematic consideration of the causes and characteristics of "domestic disorder" in the nineteenth century. I shall, as might be expected, discuss the Taiping rebellion in greater detail than any other uprisings; in doing so, I cannot avoid describing Taiping ideology and institutions in terms which will be clearer when the reader has also confronted my comments later in this essay.

The period of rebellion which is being examined here may be said to begin with the White Lotus uprisings which raged and sputtered in the mountainous border areas of Hupei, Szechwan, and Shensi provinces in north and west China from 1796 to 1804, and possibly involved as many as 300,000 rebels in scattered bands at its peak (if we accept the reports of the officials sent to pacify the rebellion). Local outbreaks at the lower end of the hierarchy of dissidence, repeated Muslim uprisings in Central Asia, unrest among other minority populations, and a major rebellion on Taiwan (1786-1787) occurred even during the apogee of the Manchu dynasty in the eighteenth century. The White Lotus rebellion, was, however, the first major disorder to occur inside China proper since the suppression of the Revolt of the Three Feudatories (1674-1681) which marked the real completion of the Manchu conquest of China. This watershed, between the era of relative internal peace during most of the reigns of the K'ang-hsi, Yung-cheng, and Ch'ien-lung emperors and the troubled nineteenth century, raises questions about the sources of both order and disorder in Ch'ing China which I shall consider below.

White Lotus Rebellion

The center of the rebellion was the mountainous watershed between the Yellow and Yangtze rivers, a border area formed by western Hupei, eastern Szechwan, and southwest Shensi which had suffered heavily from the late-Ming rebellions of Li Tzu-ch'eng and Chang Hsien-chung. Offical encouragement of migration had achieved a substantial repopulation by the early eighteenth century, but the flow of newcomers continued and spread even to very marginal highland areas. This region thus had a relatively poor economic base, a large part of its population were new settlers whose communities had not developed strong kinship and political institutions, and government

5

control (through pao-chia and other traditional means) could not be as effective as in more stable areas of longer settlement. It is precisely in such a socially uncohesive "frontier" environment that a salvational religious cult might establish a strong foothold, by meeting local needs for mutual aid and through its Buddhist chiliastic message.

Heretical sects like the White Lotus Society (Pai-lien chiao) existed just on the edge of legality, sometimes tolerated by local officials but never free of the threat of repression. In the specific case of the White Lotus, the sect's heterodox religion was combined with a Ming restorationist, anti-Ch'ing political program. It is difficult to determine at this remove the degree to which the heretical sect was only a cover for the political movement, but that the two were intertwined was important in enlarging the appeal of the sect beyond its original lower class adherents, and permitting it in some instances to infiltrate local government and local self-defense forces.

The outbreak of actual rebellion in the spring of 1796 seems to have resulted from clashes between local officials and their underlings and members of the sect, the former either seeking some reward for their toleration or engaging in haphazard extortions. There is no evidence of a planned and coordinated uprising throughout the three-province border area, nor of coordinated strategic efforts to win and hold territory after the uprising began. In this last respect the White Lotus very much resembled the Nien bands of the mid-nineteenth century. Until about the turn of the century the scattered rebel forces were able to defeat the imperial battalions--Banners and Green Standard--sent to suppress them. In part their success was a function of corruption in the Ch'ing military hierarchy during the last years of the Ch'ien-lung emperor when Ho-shen continued in power. It was due also to White Lotus control of or influence in village local defense forces before the government had developed a strategy to deprive them of this resource. As important as anything else was the effectiveness of the White Lotus guerrilla tactics; their mobile bands remained out of the reach of the generally passive tactics of the regular Ch'ing military formations.

Although the White Lotus had substantial popular support in the beginning, it was not invariably based on firm ideological commitment. Many of the destitute who swelled the rebel forces were themselves

refugees from incendiary White Lotus attacks on their villages.
There was, in other words, an ambiguity about some of the rebels:
the line between antidynastic political rebellion and nonpolitical banditry was at times a blurred one.   The roving bands, moreover, did
not create a government which might formally challenge the Ch'ing
with a rival dynastic claim.   As evidenced by the sanguinary title
"Red Lotus Society" which was widely applied to them, the imperial
troops were, if anything, even more brutal toward the local population in whose midst the White Lotus thrived.

After the accession of the Chia-ch'ing emperor to effective
power in 1799, Ho-shen and his supporters were purged, and more
effective Manchu commanders and troops--from outside the Great
Wall where the Banners' martial tradition had been less subject to
decay--were directed against the rebels.   This stiffening of the
regular army was accompanied by the widespread employment of a
strategic hamlet program and the recruitment of local militia under
official supervision.   "Strengthening the walls and clearing the
countryside" (chien-pi ch'ing-yeh), as it was called, was directed
to depriving the rebels of food and recruits by collecting the peasantry into walled villages and removing all food supplies from the
surrounding countryside.   From the village populations militia (t'uan-
lien) totaling in the tens of thousands were organized to maintain
local security, and more mobile mercenary units (hsiang-yung) num-
bering about 17,000 men in 1802 were recruited to pursue the rebels.
As a result of these measures, and promises of leniency to rank and
file dissidents, the dynasty was able to turn the tide after 1801.

The nine years of fighting, from 1796 to 1804 in five provinces,
had, according to one estimate, forced the court to spend some 120
million taels of silver, an amount totally out of proportion to the
actual size of the rebellion.   It must I think be taken as a token of
the exhaustion of the Ch'ing political system by the end of the Ch'ien-
lung period that corruption on this scale could occur.   The dynasty's
prestige as much as its treasury was damaged by this uprising which
ushered in the new century, a grim foreboding of the decades of
trouble yet to come.

The early years of the nineteenth century were marked by what
appears to be an accelerated incidence of rebellion.   These outbreaks,
although numerous, were still limited in scope and rarely reached or

sustained themselves for long at level 5 in our hierarchy of dissidence. The list is not complete, but among others note the following: outbreaks among the Miao minority populations in Kweichow, Hunan, and Szechwan in 1795-1796 and 1799; the infestation of the southeast coast between 1800-1811 by a pirate fleet of 100 or more vessels and reputedly 10,000 men; a revolt by provincial garrison armies in Shensi in 1806; uprisings by non-Han groups in Chinese Turkestan in 1807; outbreaks among aborigines in Szechwan in 1808; widespread activity by the T'ien-li-chiao secret society in Honan, Chihli, and Shantung in 1811-1813 which culminated in a picaresque attempt to seize the Forbidden City with the aid of dissident eunuchs while the Chia-ch'ing emperor was absent on a hunting trip to Jehol-- 20,000 adherents of the sect are said to have been killed in the suppression of the revolt; uprisings of impoverished marginal cultivators in Shensi in 1813 and 1814; revolts among the Muslim population of southwest China and Turkestan in 1818-1819, 1826-1828, and 1834- 1840; intertribal conflict between Tibetans and Mongols in Kokonor in 1822-1823 which required substantial Ch'ing intervention; unrest among the Yao people in Hunan and Szechwan in 1831 and 1834; revolts inspired by secret societies in Kweichow, Kwangtung, and Hunan throughout the 1830s and 1840s; and additional Muslim unrest in 1845-1846.

Short-lived, and concentrated among the non-Han minority populations on the fringes of China proper, these rebellions were put down inefficiently and at a considerable cost, but for all that with relative ease. Not so the great rebellions of the 1850s, 1860s, and 1870s whose effects were nationwide and which came very near to toppling the dynasty.

The Taiping Rebellion

Between 1850 and 1864 the Taiping Kingdom of Heavenly Peace contested with regular imperial forces and newly recruited provincial armies for control of the heart of China--the provinces of Hupei, Hunan, Anhwei, Kiangsi, Kiangsu, and Chekiang on both banks of the vital Yangtze River. Taiping expeditionary armies penetrated northward almost to the gates of Peking, while other forces campaigned in Szechwan, Kwangsi, and Kwangtung in the west and south. It is impossible even to estimate with any assurance how many hundreds of thousands (or millions) of lives were lost in this great civil war, how many millions were forced to flee from their homes as refugees from the brutalities of both contestants, how many millions of acres of cropland were devastated. Allowing for the relatively primitive weaponry in the hands of both the rebels and the imperial government, it is probable that not before the world war of 1914-1918 were conflict and carnage on such a scale seen again. From 1851 the Ch'ing dynasty faced in north China the challenge of the Nien "army" which under the impetus of early Taiping successes consolidated a multitude of hitherto fragmented rebel bands into a major threat to the regime. In its last phase the Nien absorbed substantial Taiping remnants and, thus bolstered, continued its marauding attacks until suppressed in 1868.

Hung Hsiu-ch'üan and the God-worshipping Society

The more general causes leading to the Taiping and other rebellions will be discussed later. Here it is my intention to describe the immediately precipitating events, and the principal human actors in the first part of this sometimes incredible drama. Economic stagnation, political exhaustion, the spread of local disorder, clashing lineages and ethnic groups, the impact of the foreigner, secret societies and heretical sects--all these converged in the fifth decade of the nineteenth century in the person of Hung Hsiu-ch'üan, the founder and prophet of the Heavenly Kingdom of Great Peace. Hung was born on January 1, 1814 in the village of Hua-hsien, thirty miles north of the city of Canton. His family were Hakka (a cultural-linguistic minority population which is further characterized below) "middle peasants," apparently not without some local standing as the father, Hung Ching-yang, was the headman of a group of villages. Hung's family (probably, more accurately, his lineage) was able to provide him with a classical education, and the young man demonstrated some competence along these lines by passing the qualifying examination for the lowest level civil service examination at age twelve (1825). Four times in the next twenty years he sat for the sheng-yuan degree at Canton--in 1827, 1836, 1837, and 1843--each time without success. It is unlikely that objectively Hung fared worse than the large number of other hopeful scholars who did not make it into the small quota of successful examinees and thus start down the traditional road to fame and wealth. It is certain that his psychological and political responses to his repeated failures were unusally intense and had a momentous outcome. During his second trip to Canton in 1836, Hung on two occasions listened to missionaries preaching through interpreters on the streets of the city, and accepted from the evangelists a set of pamphlets which he is said not to have read at that time. These bore the title Ch'üan-shih liang-yen [Good words to admonish the age; Canton 1832] and consisted of biblical quotations, mainly from the Old Testament as translated by the pioneer Protestant missionary Robert Morrison, and shor sermons by Liang A-fa, Milne's first convert and the compiler of the work. Hung on this visit to Canton was also exposed to lectures by a famous local scholar, Chu Tz'u-chi (1807-1882), on the Kung-yang Commentary and the "Li-yün" and "Ta-t'ung" chapters of the Li-chi [Book of rites]--central books in the utopian subtradition of Confucian thought.

The shock of Hung's third failure to win the coveted sheng-yuan title precipitated a severe nervous breakdown in 1837. According to the orthodox Taiping version as transcribed by the missionary Theodore Hamberg from the account of Hsiu-ch'üan's cousin, Hung Jenkan, during his illness Hung Hsiu-ch'üan experienced marvellous visions. The following is an excerpt:

At first, when his eyes were closed, he saw a dragon, a tiger, and a cock entering his room, and soon after, he observed a great number of men, playing upon musical instruments, approaching with a beautiful sedan-chair, in which they invited him to be seated, and then carried him away. . . . Sui-tshuen, in company with a great number of virtuous and venerable old men, among whom he remarked many of the ancient sages, entered a large building, where they opened his body with a knife, took out his heart and other parts, and put in their place others, new and of a red colour. Instantly when this was done, the wound closed, and he could see no trace of the incision which had been made.

Afterwards, they entered another large hall, the beauty and splendour of which was beyond description. A man, venerable in years, with golden beard, and dressed in a black robe, was sitting in an imposing attitude upon the highest place. As soon as he observed Sui-tshuen, he began to shed tears, and said, "All human beings in the whole world are produced and sustained by me; they eat my food and wear my clothing, and not a single one among them has a heart to remember and venerate me;

what is, however, still worse than that, they take of my
gifts and therewith worship demons; they purposely rebel
against me, and arouse my anger. Do thou not imitate
them. " Thereupon he gave Sui-tshuen a sword, com-
manding him to exterminate the demons, but to spare
his brothers and sisters; a seal, by which he would
overcome the evil spirits; and also a yellow fruit, to
eat which Sui-tshuen found sweet to the taste. When he
had received the ensigns of royalty from the hand of the
old man, he instantly commenced to exhort those collected
in the hall to return to their duties to the venerable old
man upon the high seat.

He then awoke from his trance, but still being under its
influence, he felt the very hairs of his head raise themselves, and suddenly seized by a violent anger, forgetting
his feebleness, put on his clothes, left his bedroom, went
into the presence of his father, and making a low bow,
said, "The venerable old man above has commanded that
all men shall turn to me, and all treasures shall flow to
me. " The sickness of Sui-tshuen continued about forty
days, and in vision he often met with a man of middle
age, whom he called his elder brother, who instructed
him how to act, accompanied him upon his wanderings
to the uttermost regions in search of evil spirits, and
assisted him in slaying and exterminating them. Sui-
tshuen also heard the venerable old man with the black
robe reprove Confucius for having omitted in his books
clearly to expound the true doctrine. Confucius seemed
much ashamed, and confessed his guilt (Theodore Hamberg, The Visions of Hung Sui-tshuen and Origin of the
Kwang-si Insurrection, Hong Kong, 1854; reprinted
Peking, 1935, pp. 9-11).

We can, I think, take the "forty days" of vision, the "shame"
of Confucius, and the like as post hoc embellishments without, however, discarding the whole affair as a fabrication. The phenomenon
of religious self-delusion is not rare, and even if the primal conver-
sion of the founder is subject to some inflation in the retelling, it
does not diminish the historical consequences of his experience. Did,
as Joseph Smith claimed, two celestial beings (God the Father and
Jesus Christ) really reveal the opening of a new Gospel dispensation

to him when he was only fourteen? Not likely, then or later; yet Smith clearly had a "vision" of genius in realizing that if the American west were to be opened in a way which would be efficient but undemoralizing, people would have to move not as individual families but as communities. Hung's movement, unlike the Mormons who wer also persecuted, was destroyed without a trace in less than twenty years. But he had a "vision" too: that successful revolt against the Ch'ing dynasty must in part at least be grounded in beliefs that were alien to the traditional social system, that could not be coopted and compromised. Also unlike Smith, whose greatest vice was alcohol, Hung seems to have become progressively more unbalanced mentally after the seizure of Nanking in 1853, with untoward consequences for his original vision. Though probably already alienated from the Manchu dynasty, Hung was not yet prepared to rebel. After his illness he went back to work as a village school teacher. Even his bitter feelings toward the examinations faded enough for him to try for a fourth time for the sheng-yuan degree. It was only after his fourth failure in 1843 that, according to Taiping legend, Hung read the pamphlets which he had received some years earlier. In the Good Words to Admonish the Age he purportedly found the key to his visions: the venerable old man was God and the middle-aged man Jesus. And together they had directed Hung, the younger brother of Jesus, to undertake the mission of realizing God's word on the Chinese earth.

To what degree Hung thought of himself as a religious leader as opposed to a political rebel at this point is impossible to determine. It may not have been pure accident that he turned to Liang A-fa's pamphlet in 1843; this was the year after the signature of the Treaty of Nanking, and just before the emperor granted formal toleration to Christianity in 1844. It is certain, however, that he turned zealously to evangelism among his relatives and neighbors and to iconoclastic acts which were not well received in the traditional community. Hung first converts were his schoolmate Feng Yün-shan (1822-1852) and his cousin Hung Jen-kan (1822-1864); like him they were teachers who had failed to pass the civil service examinations. Other relatives were also converted after a fashion, and Hung and his small band outraged the village elders by destroying "idolatrous" Confucian and ancestral tablets. In the spring of 1844, having lost his post as teacher, Hung Hsiu-ch'üan with Feng Yün-shan set out for Kuei-hsien, Kwangsi, mos likely to prospect for a more suitable place at which to evangelize and organize their Christian kingdom. There were a good many Hakka in

the Kuei-hsien area, including relatives of Hung, and in a few weeks
he and Feng had made more than a hundred converts. After seven
months, Hung returned to his native area in Kwangtung, while Feng
remained behind in Kwangsi. During 1845-1846 the former, supporting
himself again by teaching, began to produce the hymns, odes, songs,
and essays which became the principal doctrinal works of the Taiping
movement. Meanwhile Feng created, in Hung's name, the organiza-
tion--the God-worshipping Society (Pai Shang-ti hui)--which was to be
the vehicle for their rebellion.

In March and April 1847 Hung Hsiu-ch'üan and his cousin Jen-
kan spent about two months at the fundamentalist Southern Baptist mission in Canton which was headed by the Reverend Issachar J. Roberts
of Tennessee. The two for the first time read the whole Bible in the
revised translations of Medhurst and Gutzlaff which were superior to
the Morrison version, and also had an opportunity to observe the ritual
and practice of a Christian community. For Hsiu-ch'üan, this brief
experience and the Liang A-fa pamphlets were the total of his meagre
exposure to Christianity; the "heresies" which foreign missionaries
later criticized originated in Hung's grappling with this limited experience and extrapolating from it meanings that a fuller knowledge of
Christian doctrine might have avoided. In July 1847, with this much
preparation, Hsiu-ch'üan set off for Kwangsi to rejoin Feng Yün-shan.

The line between heretical religious sect and antidynastic rebellion might be easily crossed in late-Ch'ing China. To the dynasty, all
such sects were politically suspect and subject to repression; severe
persecution might force a sect into rebellion even if that had not been
its immediate aim. In the context of Kwangsi in the late 1840s, just
such a transformation occurred, and the Taiping rebellion was born.
In two-and-a-half years of Hung's absence, Feng, with great organizational skill, had converted nearly 3,000 persons to the crude quasi-
Christian beliefs which he and Hung had wrung from the Liang A-fa
pamphlets. The center of his activity was the Thistle Mountain area
in Kuei-p'ing hsien where the population included many Hakkas, and
the high terrain could be easily defended. The arrival of the prophet
Hung was put to good propaganda purposes, and the God-worshipping
Society which Feng had begun spread steadily in southeast Kwangsi
and southwest Kwangtung. In this early stage the religious element
dominated. In addition to baptism, congregational worship, and an
intense moralism adapted from the Ten Commandments, the sect was

given to a militant iconoclasm which aroused opposition especially among the local elite.

By mid-1849, the God-worshippers numbered about 10,000 and had recruited an able group of top leaders. In addition to Hung and Feng, these included four men of whom we should take some note. Yang Hsiu-ch'ing (1824-1856), an almost illiterate Hakka who was a leader among the charcoal workers near Thistle Mountain, became the most important figure, next to Hung, in the Taiping movement. His apparent genius for organization put into practice the politico-military system which Feng, scholar manqué, modelled on an idealized version of the military organization of the Chou dynasty. During the absence of Hung and Feng from Kwangsi in part of 1848-1849 (why is not wholly clear), Yang apparently took the first step in the direction of challenging Hung's leadership that was to lead later to his own death and a serious leadership crisis for the Taiping movement. It may be that Yang, in the beginning, saw himself forced to claim that God could descend into the world and speak through his body while he was in a trance in order to counteract divisive tendencies within the God-worshippers caused by adherents to local spirit and medium cults When Hung and Feng returned in the summer of 1849, they gave some sanction to Yang's claims and to those of Hsiao Ch'ao-kuei, another poor but influential local Hakka leader who had joined the Society, who alleged that he was in communication with Jesus Christ. This recognition prevented fragmentation of the Society, but it gave Yang in particular an opening which he was to use with increasing provocation.

A third leader of note was Wei Ch'ang-wei, a sinicized Chuang tribesman, native of Chin-t'ien village south of the mountain area, educated, and a member of one of the wealthiest lineages in Kuei-p'ing hsien. He brought several hundred members of his lineage and extensive grain stocks with him when, after several clashes with other lineages in his village, he sought the protection of the God-worshipping Society. Shih Ta-k'ai (1831?-1863), from a Hakka village in Kuei-hsie and also well-educated, was to become an outstanding Taiping military commander. He led his entire lineage to join the God-worshippers following an interlineage clash in which they were bested by non-Hakka (Punti [pen-ti]: "native residents") adversaries.

These four, plus Hung Hsiu-ch'üan and Feng Yün-shan, became sworn brothers; together they worshipped God as the Heavenly Father and Jesus Christ as the Heavenly Elder-brother, and honored Hung Hsiu-ch'üan as the Heavenly Younger-brother. Around them developed a politico-religious sect of substantial size which consisted mainly of minority Hakka peasants and charcoal workers, some of whom had joined the Society in lineage or lineage-segment groups for protection against persecution in their struggles with majority Punti lineages. Most of the early leadership came from this group. The rest of the God-worshippers consisted of an assorted lumpen-proletariat of pirates, smugglers, demobilized soldiers, unemployed porters and convoy guards, blacksmiths, carpenters, and the like, some of whom were members of Triad secret society branches; and of Chuang, Yao, and Miao tribesmen. This was the original Kwangsi core of the Taiping rebellion, which was relatively well-indoctrinated in Hung's theology, provided the bulk of the leadership, and shaped the contours of the Taiping effort to overthrow the dynasty.

It is probable that by 1849 Hung and his lieutenants were organizing more than a heretical sect. Even if it were not yet their intention to challenge the dynasty openly, they were certainly aware that their heretical stance, their support of Hakka adherents in interlineage and intervillage feuds, and their growing numbers must soon bring official repression. Moreover, in the context of growing local disorder in Kwangsi, aggravated by the severe drought of 1848-1850, it is understandable that the God-worshippers should organize militia-type units and manufacture arms at least for self-defense. An armed heretical sect, identified with local minorities and the poor, and not averse to incorporating defeated secret society members into its ranks--this was an unavoidable challenge both to the local elite and to the government. Numberous clashes occurred in 1850 between the God-worshippers (and their Hakka and outlaw supporters) on one side and gentry-organized militia backed by government troops on the other. These escalated to the point where Hung and Yang Hsiu-ch'ing, who now commanded the Society's armed forces, in the fall of 1850 ordered a general mobilization of the God-worshippers and their concentration at Chin-t'ien at the southern base of Thistle Mount. Many came with their entire families or lineages, selling their land and other property--in some cases burning their houses--and placing the proceeds in a "sacred treasury" from which all were to be supplied. These were signs of an irrevocable commitment to the cause, of a whole people rising in arms.

Even before the general mobilization, Feng Yün-shan had elaborated a scheme of military organization into which to absorb the mobilized God-worshippers, basing it on an idealized Confucian version of what purportedly had been the Chou dynasty military administration. This became the basis for the--mostly unrealized--Taiping ideal of the unity of civilian, military, and religious institutions which will be discussed below. By late 1850 Feng had ceded actual comman to Yang Hsiu-ch'ing; Yang took charge of the able-bodied males who were segregated on arrival and assigned to specific military units. In defiance of the Manchu custom of shaving the forehead, the God-worshippers let theirs grow unshaven (hence the government epithet for them: "Long Hair Bandits"). Separate camps were organized for females and dependents; no family life was permitted nor any sexual relations. In effect the noncombatants were held as hostages to guarantee the loyalty and discipline of the rank and file soldiers.

The die was cast at Chin-t'ien in the winter of 1850-1851. Clashes with government troops took place in November and December, in which the God-worshippers performed well. On January 1, 1851, the imperial forces launched a general assault against the (variously estimated as 10,000 to 30,000) rebels in the Chin-t'ien area, and were badly beaten. In the flush of victory, on January 11, 1851, Hung formally proclaimed the establishment of the Heavenly Kingdom of Great Peace (T'ai-p'ing t'ien-kuo), a new dynasty challenging Manchu rule, and himself assumed the title of Heavenly King. (T'ien-wang).

The Road to Nanking

Two years and two months after the formal proclamation of the Heavenly Kingdom of Great Peace, on March 20, 1853, the city of Nanking fell to the rebel armies. Until its reconquest in 1864 it was to be the Taiping capital. Dominating the lower Yangtze valley, its thick city wall thirty miles in length and bristling with 15,000 battlements, rich itself and surrounded by some of the richest agricultural land in China, capital of the empire in years gone by, Nanking was a fabulous prize. How could the God-worshippers of Chin-t'ien have reached such dizzy heights? The incapacity of their opponents, the appeal of their program, their tactics and discipline, these brought the Taipings to Nanking.

After the victory at Chin-t'ien in January 1851, the Taipings still faced 30,000 government troops who outnumbered and surrounded them. Their escape from encirclement in the summer of 1851 was made possible by dissension among the government leaders. On September 25, 1851, the Taipings took the city of Yung-an (present-day Meng-shan) sixty miles northeast of Thistle Mountain, the first walled city they occupied. Hemmed in again at Yung-an, the rebels recruited among the local population and increased their numbers to 40,000, about half of whom were combatants. During the lull at Yung-an the Taipings also elaborated the politico-military structure which had been initiated at Chin-t'ien, and published many of what were to be the principal doctrinal books of the Taiping movement (including Hung's writings from earlier years).

In April 1852 the Taiping armies broke out of the beseiged Yung-an, badly defeated the imperial armies under the Manchu general Wu-lan-t'ai, and began to march northward toward Hunan. The fighting was bitter and losses were heavy on both sides (including for the Taipings the death of Feng Yün-shan), but the Green Standard battalions proved unable to stem the rebel advance. The only real defeat they sustained before reaching the Yangtze was not at the hands of the regular army, but from Hunan militia under the leadership of Chiang Chung-yuan. These gentry-led volunteers, an earnest of the nemesis that Tseng Kuo-fan would later develop, in June 1852 ambushed and killed thousands of rebel soldiers attempting to cross the Hsiang river en route to Changsha, the Hunan provincial capital.

On the way to the Yangtze and especially as they moved down that major waterway toward Nanking, the Taipings were much aided by the skilled boatsmanship of bands of river pirates who had joined their cause. For many of these the alliance was a brief one; but at least one leader, Lo Ta-kang, brought several thousand of his followers with him and served the Taiping cause brilliantly until his death several years after the capture of Nanking. Lo had been a member of the Triad secret society which he left to accept the puritanical discipline of the Taiping camp. Although the Taipings sometimes cooperated closely with the Triads and similar groups as they moved northward, Taiping religious monotheism and the strictness of rebel discipline prevented any permanent union with these traditional rebellious forces.

The explicit anti-Manchu proclamations which the Taiping leaders began issuing in the June 1852 probably helped attract the cooperation of the restorationist secret societies, as their attacks on official corruption won them recruits among the impoverished peasantry on their route of march.   One bellicose proclamation read in part:

> Behold, you multitudes, listen to our words.   We believe
> that the empire belongs to the Chinese and not to the
> Manchus.   Clothes and food are provided by the Chinese,
> not by the Manchus.   Sons and daughters and other people
> living here are subjects of the Chinese, not of the Man-
> chus.   Why should we Chinese humble ourselves to be
> their servants and slaves?
>
> The Chinese have a dignified appearance; the Manchus
> have deformed us by forcing us to shave the front of
> our heads and to wear pigtails, which make us look
> like animals.   The Chinese have their own costumes;
> the Manchus have designed barbarian clothes for us, with
> monkey hats, ignoring our cultural heritage.   China has
> her own high moral standard; the Manchus have raped
> Chinese girls, taking the pretty ones to be their con-
> cubines and female slaves.   China has her political
> and legal institutions; the Manchus have made many
> devilish laws to fetter Chinese hands and feet.   China
> has her own language; the Manchus' mandarin tends to
> replace our mother tongue and confuse our pronunciation.
> Many people displaced by floods and droughts are starving
> to death and their bones are piled in heaps; the Manchus
> pay no attention to them and let them die in order to
> keep the Chinese population small.   Furthermore the
> Manchus let avaricious and corrupt officials spread all
> over the empire to "squeeze" and improvish the people.
> Government posts can be obtained by bribery, punishments
> can be rescinded by money, and hence the rich people are
> very powerful; whereas poor men of great abilities have
> no hope for employment or promotion; they can only die
> of melancholy. (trans. in S. Y. Teng, The Taiping Re-
> bellion and the Western Powers, Oxford, 1971, p. 82).

There is little evidence that the Taipings offered a specific
social program to the poor of the districts through which they passed,
apart from a general condemnation of corrupt officialdom.   They were
however, because of the strict discipline which their leaders enforced,
more welcomed by the population than were the Ch'ing armies who we:
notorious for their ill-treatment of civilians.   Sunday worship, prohi-

bition of opium, tobacco, wine, gambling, and promiscuity, and the
obligation to maintain a common treasury rather than to benefit by
private looting--these might put off the usual secret society leader,
but they reflected a better treatment of the local people than the
latter usually experienced from armies in transit. On the basis of
their greater discipline which could win popular support for their
troops, the Taipings developed guerrilla tactics with which the Ch'ing
regular battalions, although they were better armed, could not cope.

The Taipings did not garrison the cities that they captured, but
moved on towards the Yangtze river which was reached in the winter
of 1852-1853. At this time the rebels numbered perhaps 100,000--
of whom less than half were fighting men, and at most 30,000 (including men and women) had originally joined the movement in Kwangsi
and Kwangtung. Given the size of the imperial forces which pursued
them, they were still few, not really enough to establish their Heavenly Kingdom. After taking Wuchang, the capital of Hupei, in January
1853--this key city was to change hands several times in the next de-
cade--the Taipings for the first time forcibly conscripted a civilian
population into their ranks. The efficacy of the original religious
appeal was too limited to be relied upon exclusively, in view of the
larger ends now in mind. Some attempts were made then and later
to offer religious instruction and indoctrination of the populations of
newly conquered territories, but with limited success. This is a
major factor in explaining the almost total disappearance of the
Taiping movement (except for remnants who joined the Nien) after
the recapture of Nanking in 1864.

The final push toward Nanking began in February 1853, the
proponents of continuing northward to Peking having been out-argued.
Several hundred thousand rebels (including the Wuchang conscripts)
set out eastward, some by river in 20,000 boats and others by land.
Along the way, the looted cities of Kiukiang and Anking provided large
quantities of silver, weapons including cannon, and plentiful food supplies. Nanking held out for thirteen days before its walls were
breached by tunneling and explosives. Its Chinese civilian population,
men and women, was conscripted into the Taiping forces after the
conquest; Manchu soldiers and civilians--20,000 or more of them--
were executed. A decision came quickly that the Taipings would go
no further; Nanking would be the Heavenly Capital. The forward
momentum of the great armed migration from south China was pre-
cipitately halted. Historians have generally considered this to have

been a major strategic mistake; Peking might have been taken in the
first months of 1853, before the dynasty recovered from the shock of
the Taipings' early victories.   By mid-year, when an expeditionary
force was launched against the Ch'ing capital, it was too late.   But
what was this New Jerusalem on the southeastern bank of the Yangtze
river to be?

Taiping Ideology

I have already quoted a blustering anti-Manchu document; it is
evident that racial or ethnic hostility--a quasi-nationalism, because
the nineteenth-century Manchus were no longer really "foreigners" or
"barbarians"--was one central component of the Taiping ideology.   At
first glance there is little that is new here, similar phrasings had
occurred in rebellions earlier in the Ch'ing dynasty. ' But note that
the usual accompaniment of Buddhist ideas (as in the White Lotus
case) was absent, as is the Ming restorationist theme that characterized the secret societies' opposition to the Manchus. Hung Hsiu-
ch'üan had no interest in restoring the Ming dynasty or any dynasty,
merely because it was Chinese and not "barbarian."   The Taiping
Heavenly Kingdom (T'ien-kuo) was to be something else again: a
transcendental Christian monarchy which starkly challenged the Confucian conception of the state as a condominium of the emperor and
the literati-bureaucracy.   Christianity, as it were, made possible an
option which imperial Confucianism had always been able to temper
if not suppress entirely: an omnipotent ruler sanctioned by a single
universal God who could realize the Confucian literati's worst night-
mare--rule in the interest not of the Confucian "general will" but in
the service of the emperor's raison d'état (in this case of his theocratic messianism).   In a truly "Legalist" state what independent
role could there be for the Confucian cultural integuement which the
gentry elite had created and transmitted and which, through the
emperor, the bureaucracy, and the examination system, had legitimized themselves as the social and political ruling class of imperial
China? This Taiping challenge--based first on the idea of a monarchy that was not in part at least a creature of those who served
it in office or in their studies--was compounded by the circumstance
that the Taiping outlook was shaped not just by Christianity, but
equally by a Chinese utopian tradition whose egalitarian component
ran directly counter to the fundamentally hierarchical tendency of
mainstream Confucian thought and society.

I state all this first in so abstract a manner because it is questionable that /the Taiping leaders had a clear intelligence of the dynamics of the nineteenth-century Chinese society in these terms, that they really attacked the Confucian system because they understood the critical role of the Confucian-educated gentry who dominated local society by their wealth and prestige and from among whom, via the civil service examinations, came the chief functionaries of the state. / My point is not that the Taipings were social and political revolutionaries as we understand this in the post-French Revolution Western world, but that their contest with the Manchu dynasty was nevertheless more portentous than any other domestic challenge faced by the imperial state. Taiping victory would not have meant, as some optimistic Marxist historians have asserted, the establishment of some kind of peasant communism. But conceivably it would have ruptured the particular form of gentry society which, through successive dynastic changes, had continued to underlie the Chinese state system. The closest analogy that I can, hesitatingly, suggest is the process whereby the Russian autocracy, by the "binding," or enserfment, into compulsory state service of all classes, from the peasantry to the gentry, achieved by the time of Peter I a degree of national cohesion and commitment to a rational legal order which had been accomplished in Western Europe by civil society itself with much smaller state intervention. Something on this pattern might, if one stretches his imagination, be seen to have been the agenda that a victorious Taiping monarchy would have faced. Ch'ing China, like Muscovite Russia, was "backward" compared to the modernizing, bourgeois states of the West, and in the nineteenth century context it was exposed to even a greater challenge than Peter felt in the late seventeenth. Cannot Hung Jen-kan's New Work for Aid of Government, on which I shall comment further below, possibly be seen as providing the intellectual basis for precisely such a "nation-building" process?

Admittedly the foregoing remarks are at best speculation. / The Confucian elite, in any case, knew that the Taipings represented a threat to themselves,) as the linchpin of Chinese society, of unprecedented seriousness. As we shall see, they rallied almost to a man to save the dynasty and their society. But the Taiping version of Christianity, which provided the élan that held the rebel movement together, was peculiarily dependent on the religious fervour of the original core of God-worshippers from Kwangsi. And this paradoxically contributed to the inability of the Taiping ideological challenge to be genuinely revolutionary in our contemporary sense of not only rejecting the present, evil world and promising in its place the millenium, but also specifically elaborating the way that the new society would be brought into existence (e.g., political and social programs, a system of organization, a doctrine about the transfer of power). The social psychology of the persecuted Hakka communities out of which the God-worshippers grew made them unusually receptive to the chosen-people imagery and the militant messianism that Feng and Hung brought to them from their own limited acquaintance with the Bible. It also apparently confirmed them as outsiders in the new context of Nanking as they had been outsiders--Hakka (k'o-chia, "guest people")--in Kwangsi, and Kwangtung. The Taiping leadership and the core of true believers, protected by the great wall that encircled Nanking, were in effect cut off, alienated from the rural areas of the Yangtze provinces for whose control they fought. They were, to put it yet another way, psychologically as well as politically unable to penetrate to the rural society beneath the hsien level and remake it to their own revolutionary design by supplanting the traditional leadership of the Confucian gentry.

/ The religious convictions of Hung Hsiu-ch'üan and other early Taiping leaders were certainly genuine, although they appeared distorted or heretical to foreign Christians. Hung himself paid no attention to charges of heterodoxy since he never grasped his divergence from orthodoxy. His understanding of theology was narrowly circumscribed by Morrison's inadequate biblical translations which he had found in Liang A-fa's pamphlets. He had to work a lot out for himself, and the results as Hung's annotations on the Old and New Testaments demonstrate were sometimes the ramblings of a madman. / Note the following on the concept of the Trinity:

> There is only one Supreme God, Christ is the First Son
> of God. The Son was born of the Father, originally one
> and only one body. But the Father is the Father; the
> Son, the Son; one in two, and two in one. As to the
> Holy Spirit or the Eastern King [i.e., Yang Hsiu-ch'ing],
> Almighty God issued an edict appointing him to be the
> Spirit. The Eastern King is a beloved Son of God, and,
> together with the Great Elder Brother and Myself, was
> born of the same Mother. Before the beginning of Heaven
> and Earth, all three of us were of the same Father, as
> the Heavenly Father God is the one and only True God.

The one and only True God says: "Besides Myself,
thou shalt have no other gods." The Holy Ghost is
really God. If there should be another Holy Ghost,
there would be another Divine Being (trans. in J. C.
Cheng, Chinese Sources for the Taiping Rebellion,
1850-1864, Hong Kong, 1963, p. 88).

/ Taiping sectarian Christianity took from the Old Testament the
idea of a transcendental, personal God who could be appealed to with-
out priestly intervention. While this conception contrasted sharply
with the immanent Heaven (t'ien) of Confucianism, the Taiping Holy
Family preserved echoes of the Chinese family system:/ the Heavenly
Father and His Wife; the Heavenly Elder Brother and His Wife; the
Heavenly Younger Brother and Savior for China, and His Wives.
From the Old Testament, too, came a militant iconoclasm, a strict
Sabbatarianism, a central place for the Ten Commandments, and the
concept of a God of wrath who would punish transgressors. From the
New Testament the Taipings took the idea that God was the god of all
men, not just of the Jews and Chinese; the basic facts of Christ's
life, such practices as baptism and the Lord's Prayer; and a belief
in the redemption from sin. I The Taipings were also strong on public worship, the chanting of hymns, and grace before meals, and for
the masses (but not the leaders) they insisted on a strict puritanism
with respect to opium, tobacco, and sex.I The principal omissions
from Taiping Christianity--leaving aside distortions additional to the
trinitarian discussion quoted above--were the sacrament of Holy Com-
munion, that part of Christianity associated with the quintessential
message of love in Christ's teachings, and the ideas of a church and
a distinct clergy.

I Hung's attraction to Christianity was not only because of the
obvious power of its message for him, but also as I have noted because it was a means of bypassing and undermining the Confucian
system. Hence the claims in Taiping writings that the Shang-ti [Lord-
on-high] whom the Chinese worshipped in pre-Confucian times was in
fact Jehovah, the God of the Hebrews; that Taiping Christianity was a
return to the original faith of China which the West had equally known
and accepted; and that China was the locus of the God's latest revela-
tion. Both the universalistic and the incipient nationalistic overtones
in such statements could spell disaster for Confucianism, for a system of ideas which identified Chinese culture as Culture.

Christianity also contributed to the force of the Taiping millenarian outlook, that is, to the belief that a totally new world of grea
happiness, good government, and freedom from wickedness would replace the depraved Ch'ing state and society. As Hung's biblical com
mentary stated it: "Both in Heaven and on earth is the Heavenly
Kingdom of the Divine Father. Do not imagine that it refers solely
to the Heavenly Kingdom in Heaven. Thus the Great Elder Brother
formerly issued an edict foretelling the coming of the Heavenly Kingdom soon, meaning that the Heavenly Kingdom would come into being
on earth" (trans. in J.C. Cheng, Chinese Sources, p. 83). The
greatest part of Taiping utopian ideology, however, and the blueprint
for the actual institutions that were to implement it, had their origin
in Chinese tradition--not the mainstream of imperial Confucianism,
a heterodox utopian tradition that had surfaced several times before
China's long history. Two related observations are in order before
considering that tradition. First, Hung and Feng and several others
of the early Taiping leaders, although they failed in the civil service
examinations, had received an education in the Chinese classical lite
ature. It is not, therefore, surprising that, while they rejected imperial Confucianism, they remained Confucian enough to conceive of
salvation on earth as necessarily achieved through political organization. Second, in view of the fact that little of the new society was
ever put into practice, it is possible that their utopianism was mostl
a mobilizational device to generate the superhuman efforts among the
adherents without which the overthrow of the dynasty could never be
effected.

I have already noted that Hung in his early twenties had become
acquainted with the utopian subtradition in Chinese classical thought.
This found its expression in a number of texts which permitted of
millenarian visions potentially subversive to the imperial order. The
"Li-yün" [Evolution of rites] section of the Li-chi [Book of rites],
a syncretic Han dynasty compilation, describes an "age of Great Har
mony" (ta-t'ung) in the past in which "the world was shared by all
alike," and men were not concerned only with the aggrandizement of
their own families. (This is clearly a Taoist influence in the text.
K'ang Yu-wei revived the concept in the late nineteenth century, and
Mao Tse-tung has used the term ta-t'ung as the equivalent of "communism" itself.) Similar themes referring to the Taiping adherents
as members of one family that shared both material possessions and
God's love recur in Taiping doctrinal writings. The attempts to seg-
regate the sexes during the march on Nanking and even after the con

quest of that city, which had other motives as well, along with some tentative moves in the direction of more equal treatment of women, might possibly be construed as intended to alter or replace the traditional kinship system. Evidence of both intention and practice is, however, quite scanty in this matter.

The Taiping removal of utopia from the primitive past to the millenarian future was supported by the concept of Three Ages which appears in the Kung-yang chuan [Kung-yang commentary on the Spring and Autumn Annals]. This text enumerates an evolution from the Age of Disorder, through the Age of Order, to the Age of Great Peace (T'ai-p'ing) in which a condition similar to "Great Harmony" would be achieved. Possibly too great attention has been given to the ambiguously egalitarian purport of the two texts just described. The T'ien-ch'ao t'ien-mou chih-tu [Land system of the Heavenly Dynasty; 1853], which outlines the ideal forms of Taiping political, economic, military, and religious institutions, draws very heavily from the non-egalitarian, idealized, almost compulsively symmetrical summary of Chou dynasty society found in the Chou-li [Rites of Chou; a Han dynasty text]. Since the Chou as there depicted never existed, I suppose that it may be termed a utopia too, but a distinctly hierarchical and bureaucratized one.

Taiping Institutions

What kind of institutions were established on the basis of the ideology I have summarized? How was the Heavenly Kingdom organized and administered? Two important distinctions should be made in any reply to these questions: first, between ideals and practice; and second, between Nanking, the Heavenly Capital, and other territories which the Taipings controlled for various lengths of time. The two distinctions are related, for practical military exigencies severely limited the ability of the Taipings to put their ideals into practice outside of the capital and its immediate environs where their rule was secure for a decade. It may almost be said that after 1856 there was no unified history of the Taiping movement, because at best Nanking maintained only loose authority over the shifting areas that its armies fought to dominate.

The government in Nanking under the Heavenly King Hung Hsiu-ch'üan gave the appearance of an elaborate centralized bureaucracy, in

practice it was often more nearly a congeries of competing royal
appanages. Until 1856, the chief administrator and most powerful
leader after Hung was Yang Hsiu-ch'ing who bore the title Eastern
King. Yang's central administration consisted of more than fifty
departments and agencies all with titles taken directly from the Chou
period. Yang, however, also had a court of his own, and a personal
administrative and military staff. So too did the other surviving earl
rebel leaders who like Yang were endowed with royal titles (Northern
King, Wei Ch'ang-hui; Assistant King, Shih Ta-k'ai). Other kings or
princes were created as the years passed; before 1855, there were
only seven; toward the end of the Taiping dynasty, they numbered
more than 2,000. For the more important nobility, their titles were
a recognition of some degree of autonomous military power. It was
not quite a "feudal" system, but after the death of Yang in 1856 the
administration was only very loosely held together. Life in Hung's
court and those of the principal kings was luxurious, and polygamous;
the Heavenly King apparently had a harem of several dozen "wives."
In the first year or so Hung performed his role of prophet well enoug
and a large number of doctrinal works, most importantly The Land Sy
tem of the Heavenly Dynasty, were issued of which he was probably t
author. (Forty-four official Taiping books and pamphlets were publish
between 1853 and 1862.) Increasingly, thereafter, he withdrew into hi
palace and left practical political matters first to Yang Hsiu-ch'ing, a
then after 1856 to competing factions of his relatives and supporters.
There is, in fact, very little credible information about Hung's life ar
ideas after the conquest of Nanking. Perhaps the mental instability
manifested in his early visions reappeared in a more advanced form
and progressively undermined his ties to the reality he had created

[1]As outlined in The Land System of the Heavenly Dynasty, the
Taiping new society was to combine in one hierarchy all political, ecc
nomic, religious, and social institutions. The basic unit of this ideal
system was a group of twenty-five families under the leadership of a
"sergeant" (liang ssu-ma, a term like those of other Taiping officials
taken from the Chou-li). The ssu-ma was to serve as civil administrator and judge, preside at religious ceremonies and daily worship,
act as platoon leader in time of war, collect grain from the twenty-
five families in his charge, and supervise their "sacred treasury" (or
public storehouse). Starting from this basic module, the entire societ
was to be organized in a symmetrical pattern echoing the Chou of old.
A Taiping army, for example, consisted of 500 platoons (each of 25
men under the command of a liang ssu-ma), organized into 125 com-

panies, 25 batallions, and 5 divisions--a total of 13,156 including the officers at each level. The army commanders, in theory, were also to be the next highest civil administrative officers under the Taiping equivalent of a district (hsien) magistrate.

It is generally accepted that a large part of the Taiping early military success was attributable to the good organization of the rebel armies and hence their responsiveness to command. We may take this as evidence that a military hierarchy, possibly patterned on the ideal just described, was implemented at least on some occasions. For the rest, with the partial exception of Nanking itself, although the evidence is very scanty, its present weight supports the conclusion that neither twenty-five family groups, nor "common treasuries," nor local churches ever materialized. There is evidence that prefectural and district officials were fairly regularly appointed for areas occupied after 1853, and that places outside of the immediate war zone were occasionally closely administered even below the hsien level. As an overall summary, however, I suggest that Taiping administration outside of Nanking normally consisted of the superimposition of military garrisons upon a largely unchanged local society which remained intact and impenetrable for the purposes of political organization--though not immune from conscription or, as we shall see, taxation. The garrisons themselves varied in the degree to which their commanders and troops were bound to the ideology of Hung Hsiu-ch'üan and amenable to direction from Nanking.

In Nanking, in the early years of the Heavenly Kingdom, apparently some "communal" organization was accomplished. Handicraft workers were organized into groups by trade in order to insure adequate supplies of weapons and other necessities for the military and luxuries for the kings. Some segregation of the sexes, at least among the original God-worshippers, was maintained until 1855. The booty of war in the early years was concentrated in a "sacred treasury" for the public benefit. And foreign observers reported a rudimentary system of public supply, but it is not clear whether this was only a dole to the poor or a more comprehensive effort. Little of all of this was left after 1860, as the Ch'ing military noose began to tighten around the Heavenly Capital.

/The radical redistribution of land in amounts proportionate to the number of persons in each family prescribed in The Land System of the Heavenly Dynasty we must take as an expression of Taiping ideals rather than practice. It was not implemented anywhere, and thus the argument for describing the Taiping movement as a kind of "peasant communism" rests only on a document of eight folio pages which was never considered a program for action. Providing as it did equal land allotments to male and female alike, the Taiping plan in this respect went a step beyond the "land equalization" traditions of earlier dynasties which had preponderantly favored men. Some resonance from the Christian faith in the universal Fatherhood of God possibly underlay this support of equality for women; as well as, no doubt, the influence of the Hakka women from Kwangsi who often worked in the fields with men and enjoyed greater equality than other Chinese women. The Taipings forbade footbinding, concubinage, and the purchase of brides, although, as I have noted, concubinage wa as it traditionally had been, practiced by the Taiping elite. How much in fact the status of women was improved under Taiping rule is uncertain; probably not much, although the idea was evidently present among the original core of God-worshippers in Nanking.

In general, scholars in Taiping territory were well-treated personally, and a system of civil service examinations was instituted in 1853 to recruit a bureaucracy in the traditional manner. The examinations, based entirely on Taiping publications, do not seem to have been very successful in this regard; the paucity of educated men dedicated to the Taiping ideals, must be seen as a major factor in the inability of the rebels to challenge the traditional elite for the domination of local society--even in areas which the Taipings controlled militarily. Two options presented themselves if the rebels sought to secure a firm base in local society from which to challenge the regime in power. The first was to coopt or supplant the existing local power structure without altering basic economic and social institutions. The second was to organize the rural masses into a political instrument with which--village by village--to smash existing institutions and eliminate the social roles played by the old elite; and then to reorganize rural society on a new basis under rebel auspices. Neither was accomplished by the Taipings. There were relatively few gentry recruits to their cause on the route to Nanking, and few were produced by their examination system. The Taiping ideological and political threat to Confucianism, moreover, made most of the existing elite, in and out of office, implacable enemies of the Heavenly Kingdom. Without sufficient and qualified cadres, Taiping control over rural areas was no less superficial than the Ch'ing system. And social revolution primarily in the interests of the peasantry was not what the Taiping movement was primarily about.

Additional support for the last preceding statement is provided by the Taiping tax system. On the march to Nanking, the Taiping armies had burned land deeds and rent records, this being one way of recruiting peasants to their cause. After the conquest of Nanking, private ownership of land was in fact unchanged (and even protected), and the Ch'ing procedures for tax collection were followed without significant change. In face of the necessity to raise funds for large-scale military operations, no tampering with the traditional fiscal base could be contemplated. Indeed, in many cases even the Ch'ing tax collectors remained, i.e., the local gentry who had long inserted themselves into the taxing process and now, as it were, remitted to the Taipings as they had to the Ch'ing in exchange for a de facto guarantee of their economic and social status. The Ch'ing rates of taxation were, however, not necessarily followed. Military commanders exercised considerable autonomy with respect both to the amount of the land tax (in the common form of grain requisitions) levied in the areas under their control, and to the proportion of the collection that was remitted to the control of the central government. (The only revenue collected directly by the Nanking government came from duties levied on trade on the Yangtze river.)

Internal Dissension and New Leadership

The year 1856 marked the peak of Taiping power and military success; it was also a year of bloody dissension within the Taiping leadership which had far-reaching consequences for the survival of the rebellion. I have already noted the immense preoccupation with titles and honors among the Taiping leadership, and the existence of potentially discordant factions organized around the courts of the several kings. The fratricide of the fall of 1856 was touched off by the ambitions of Yang Hsiu-ch'ing whose power and pretensions to speak in the voice of God had grown as Hung became increasingly immured in his palace. Yang's plot to usurp Hung's position became known to the latter who in turn prompted Wei Ch'ang-wei, the Northern King, and the important military commander Ch'in Jih-kang to assassinate Yang. In bloody massacres that lasted for days, Yang, his family and retinue, and his personal soldiers were mercilessly slaughtered. The triumphant and equally ambitious Wei now turned on his chief remaining rival, the Assistant King Shih Ta-k'ai, and massacred his family and followers, but not Shih himself who had withdrawn from Nanking with his best troops. Hung Hsiu-ch'üan, (actually the Heavenly King's relatives and entourage), alarmed by what he had set in motion, mustered enough force in Nanking to arrest Wei and Ch'in and executed them. As many as 30,000 persons, some sources claim, died in Nanking in the course of these internecine struggles.

The Taiping administrative structure was badly damaged: for all his arrogance and ambition, Yang Hsiu-ch'ing had been an able administrator. And Shih Ta-k'ai, the Taiping's most capable military leader at this time and genuinely loyal to Hung Hsiu-ch'üan, a man who might have picked up the pieces and replaced Yang, was in effect driven from the capital by Hung's brothers who feared that their influence on the monarch would be diminished. The departure, never to return, of Shih Ta-k'ai and many troops from Nanking in May 1857 on a "western expedition" was a blow to the defense of the capital area. It was also the beginning of Shih's degeneration from a militant crusader for the Taiping cause into a roving nonideological bandit whose substantial force greatly troubled both the government and the populace until his capture and execution by slicing in August 1863. With no real unified command after 1856, the Taiping movement began a process of centrifugal disintegration that was only temporarily arrested by the advent of new political and military leaders.

Hung Jen-kan, the Heavenly King's distant cousin who had been among his first converts, did not accompany the Taipings from Kwang to Nanking. Only in April 1859, was he able to travel through the im perial blockade to the Taiping capital. Within a month after his arri Jen-kan had been elevated to the highest positions in the rebel movement: with the title "Shield King" (Kan-wang) he nominally exercised powers of prime minister and commander-in-chief as Yang Hsiu-ch'in had formerly done. Jen-kan, who in the intervening years had had much contact with Protestant missionaries in Hong Kong and Shanghai (for example, as a catechist of the London Missionary Society), and had also been exposed to some "Western learning," seemed like the answer to the leadership crisis. Hsiu-ch'üan's rapid promotion of his cousin over the heads of many others who had served the rebellion from the beginning is an indication of the desperation in Nanking.

The Shield King's ascendancy, however, was brief. By 1861 the forces of decentralization and factional contention had stifled his effor to reform and refurbish the Taiping regime. Jen-kan's ideas and pre gram were presented in a document, New Work for Aid in Governmen (Tzu-cheng hsin-pien, late 1859) which presaged much of the Ch'ing "self-strengthening" effort of the last decades of the nineteenth century. Jen-kan drew attention to the experience of other countries, and advocated that the Taipings promote railroads, steamships, modern banks, the development of mining, post offices, and newspapers, i.e., the "modernization" with which some strains of nineteenth century Protestantism also identifed themselves. He was furthermore concerned that the Taiping administration be rationalized and centralized, again on the model of the foreign countries from which his missionary acquaintenances came. Jen-kan also hoped to substitute a more conventional Protestant Christian theology for that which Hsiuch'üan had elaborated from his limited exposure to both texts and missionaries. It is a brief (25 folio pages) and frequently naive document, whose influence has been sometimes exaggerated, for the author was able to accomplish none of these goals. One may speculate, however, that in spite of the general context of ignorance and arrogance in Nanking, the New Work for Aid in Government represents better than any other rebel publication what the Taiping movement might have become if it had been successful in its struggle against the Manchu dynasty. Not peasant communism, but an étatist effort to bring China from its "backwardness" and superficial political unity to a level of "modernization" and national cohesion which could mitigate, though probably not terminate, the growing and seemingly inexorable sweep of the West into China. To be successful, such a program would have required the end of Confucianism as the intelligence of Chinese society, and a radical transformation of the relations between the bureaucratic state and the gentry who dominated local society. As I have suggested, the Taipings explicitly pursued the first of these prerequisites; the second was ever further from their reach.

Hung Jen-kan's failure to achieve a recentralization of the forces of the rebellion was manifested in his relations with the two new military leaders who emerged simultaneously with his arrival in Nanking, Ch'en Yu-ch'eng and Li Hsiu-ch'eng. They were to be the instruments of a grand military plan which Jen-kan proposed for the conquest and control of the whole of the Yangtze river valley, from Wuchang to Shanghai. As I shall note below, the attractions of the wealth of east China magnetized Li Hsiu-ch'eng and precluded his full cooperation. As in the case of Shih Ta-k'ai, the original Taiping religious fervour and commitment to the cause of realizing the Heavenly Kingdom on earth had begun to wear thin. The line between large-scale anti-dynastic banditry and chiliastic rebellion might be a faint one, easy to cross without really noticing.

+ Taiping Foreign Relations

ᐧ In view of the Taiping claim to share a universal religion with
the Western powers ("we are all sons of God and younger brothers
of Jesus Christ," went one rebel statement), it is understandable that
at first the Heavenly Kingdom appeared to the foreigners as less reluctant than the Ch'ing government to permit the expansion of foreign
trade and evangelism. The initial response of Protestant missionarie
was generally positive, and this probably influenced the diplomats as
well. Very quickly, however, the euphoria faded away, as both missionaries and consuls acquired firsthand knowledge of the rebellion
to supplement their early wishful thinking. The Taipings were not
explicitly antiforeign, though they were not without the cultural
arrogance toward the Western representatives who visited them that
also characterized their imperial rivals.ᐟ What changed foreign sym-
pathy first to cool neutrality and then to open hostility were the missionaries' discovery that the Taipings were adamant about the "blas-
phemous" version of Christianity which Hung espoused, and the
diplomats' growing appreciation that the rebels were not strong
enough to overthrow the dynasty. Direct contact between several
missionaries and the Taipings after the capture of Nanking in 1853
revealed "errors" in doctrine and practice--notably Hung Hsiu-ch'üan'
claim to be the second son of God--which diminished the earlier zeal
for the rebels. A number of missionaries who had known Hung Jen-
kan and who visited Soochow and Nanking in 1860 and 1861, notably
Joseph Edkins of the English Wesleyan mission and Griffith John of
the Episcopal mission, continued to report favorably, largely because
of assurances they received that missionaries would be permitted to
work freely in insurgent territory. The American Baptist Issachar
J. Roberts, with whom Hung Hsiu-ch'üan had studied briefly in Canton in 1847, even spent fifteen months in Nanking between October
1860 and January 1862. But the mainstream of sentiment was increasingly negative, and Roberts joined his voice to it when he broke
with Hung and the Taipings over matters of religious doctrine.

Foreign diplomatic visitors to Taiping territory included Sir
George Bonham, British plenipotentiary and governor of Hong Kong,
in April-May 1853; the French minister de Bourboulon in December
1853; the American commissioner Robert M. McLane in April 1854;
and John Bowring, Bonham's successor, in June 1854. Although the
superficial result of these missions was the adoption by the powers of
a policy of neutrality, in fact these foreign respresentatives on the w

came away with unfavorable impressions of the abilities of the Taiping leaders with whom they or their interpreter-assistants talked (Thomas Taylor Meadows, Bonham's interpreter, was more sanguine than his chief and produced one of the outstanding foreign accounts of the Taiping rebellion: The Chinese and Their Rebellions, London, 1856). And the failure of the Taiping expedition against Peking in 1853-1854 contributed importantly to Bowring's impression, for example, that in view of the gains to be anticipated from pending treaty revision negotiations with the Ch'ing court, no aid should be given to the rebels against the imperial government.

¦ Foreign neutrality was maintained until the war of 1856-1860, the Treaties of Tientsin, and the Peking Conventions had secured for the powers the increased privileges in China which they had sought. It might be argued that this policy was seen as a lever with which to extract concessions from the dynasty, which feared the possibility of foreign assistance to its domestic foe. After 1860, neutrality gave way to active but small-scale support of the defense of Shanghai and the government reconquest of east China.

The Taipings indeed had little to offer the foreigners that the latter could not coerce from the existing dynasty. The Ch'ing while it might be seen as both "bad, corrupt, and ignorant," and arrogantly asserting its superiority over the foreign barbarians, did not potentially challenge the Western powers on their own moral ground. ¦ It could not--as the Taipings someday might--question the propriety of special privileges seized by military force by one Christian state from another.

Military Strategy and Operations

On the march to Nanking, the rebel army's strategy as we have seen was not directed to holding the territories through which it passed, but to recruiting followers and capturing food and supplies. The decision to proceed to Nanking after the capture of Wuchang, rather than to move immediately against Peking before the dynasty could recover from the shock of the early Taiping victories, may itself have been a strategic error of some consequence. Once ensconced in the Heavenly Capital, the rebels' military plans called for the belated pursuit of the objective of taking the Ch'ing capital, and simultaneously sought to recover and control the Yangtze provinces which they had abandoned earlier. The success of these two primary offensive objectives depended on the ability to defend Nanking against the imperial forces which surrounded it. This last, until the very end of the rebellion, the Taipings succeeded in doing with some aplomb. While the Ch'ing regular forces encamped outside the rebel capital (the Great Camp of Kiangnan and the Great Camp of Kiangpei) might hinder the Taipings' military movements and lines of supply, they were incredibly ineffective as offensive forces. In June 1856, the Taipings literally wiped out the Great Camp of Kiangnan and killed its commander, the general Hsiang Jung. And siege was broken a second time in May 1860 by Li Hsiu-ch'eng, again with the loss of the imperial commander.

It is difficult to state why so small a force was dispatched nor ward in May 1853 for the intended conquest of Peking. Logistical pr lems undoubtedly played a part, as well as the Taiping expectation th additional forces could be recruited en route, as on the march to Na king. Still even 70-80,000 (the largest and probably much exaggerat figure suggested in the sources) were too few, and the new recruits-in northern Anhwei, for example, where locally severe famine produ many desperate peasants--were poorly equipped and supplied. The Y low river was crossed only with great losses, but the Taiping northe expedition in five months fought its way to within three miles of Tier tsin and seventy miles of Peking, before being thrown back and then progressively decimated by the Mongol general Seng-ko-lin-ch'in's cavalry the onset of a severe northern winter for which the rebel southerners were not prepared. Such remnants as survived from the Taiping expeditionary army joined with the Nien rebels of north Chin to continue to harass the government.

The simultaneous effort to reconquer Anhwei, Kiangsi, Hupei, and Hunan under the command of Shih Ta-k'ai at first proceeded mor smoothly. Tseng Kuo-fan, who was gradually putting together the el ments of the new military forces and political strategy which would eventually defeat the Taipings, was able to defend Hunan with his mi tia-based army. Between 1853 and 1856, however, the victories see sawed, and the Taipings captured and held for varying periods of tin such major strategic points as Kiukiang in Kiangsi, and the three Wuhan cities in Hupei. When Shih was recalled to the rebel capital to attack Hsiang Jung's Great Camp of Kiangnan in May 1856, the Taipings controlled all of the districts along the Yangtze for 300 mil between Wuchang and Nanking. This was the economic heartland of central China, indispensable if the Taiping regime were to survive. After 1856, however, the fratricidal dissension described above first

detained Shih and his troops in the Nanking area and then impelled
him into semiautonomous military adventures. The Ch'ing forces
under Tseng Kuo-fan's leadership consequently recovered control of
the territory west of Nanking.

In spite of temporary successes in 1858 in northern Anhwei,
the major remaining source of supply for the capital, when Hung Jen-
kan arrived in Nanking in 1859 the military situation had grossly dete-
rioated. Jen-kan's strategic response was to undertake a two-pronged
coordinated attack by armies moving westward along both banks of the
Yangtze with the aim of once more recapturing Wuchang. To provide
the facilities for this major offensive, he considered it necessary that
the east Kiangsu cities (e.g., Shanghai, Soochow, Hangchow) be conquered first--as a means of diverting Ch'ing troops from the west,
and also to provide funds and military supplies. To compensate for
the decline of Taiping naval power after 1853, Jen-kan hoped to ob-
tain armed steamers in Shanghai which would be capable of clearing
the Yangtze of enemy forces. Li Hsiu-ch'eng (1824?-1864), the
Loyal King (Chung-wang), a Kwangsi veteran who had begun as a
common soldier in the Taiping army, was given the responsibility for
the eastern expedition, at the completion of which he was to move his
troops westward along the south bank of the Yangtze parallel to Ch'en
Yu-ch'eng's forces which were deployed north of the river. Li's initial successes were brilliant: Soochow was conquered in June 1860;
Ningpo, Hangchow, and other cities soon fell to his armies (300,000
persons are reported to have starved to death during the Taiping
siege of Hangchow; both sides treated civilians, as well as their military adversaries, with enormous cruelty).

Though much of the wealthy provinces of Chekiang and Kiangsu
came under Taiping control in 1861, in fact the balance of power had
begun to shift to the imperial side. For one thing, Shanghai could no
longer be taken as it might have been in 1853; with the end of foreign
neutrality in China's great civil war (coincident with the defeat of the
dynasty in the "Second Opium War" and the enlargement of the treaty
system by the Treaties of Tientsin), foreign troops now helped defend
its city walls. Li, moreover, had become increasingly concerned with
strengthening his own position, rather than carrying out Nanking's strategy. And for the augmentation of his strength, what was better than the
riches of the lower Yangtze valley. After an irresolute effort to attack
toward the west, he withdrew his forces entirely to east China. There
he remained strong, and continued to threaten Shanghai. But the Loyal

King was less and less "revolutionary" in the areas that he controlle
the necessity to raise funds and supply food for his troops made for
increasing compromise with the gentry landlords, and for a growing
burden on the population.

Suppression of the Rebellions

What had changed most was that the troops facing the Taiping
armies were no longer primarily the demonstrably incompetent Green
Standard batallions. The Hunan Army (Hsiang-chün) which Tseng Kuo
fan had organized and Li Hung-chang's Huai Army (Huai-chün)--I sha
discuss them further below--were not only better organized, paid, an
equipped than the Ch'ing regular army, but were led by men who wei
ideologically commited to destroy the Taipings and who indoctrinated
their troops with the same spirit. Like the early Taipings, they
fought for a cause and therefore fought with more success than the
dispirited Green Standard batallions. The appointment of Tseng Kuo-
fan to the posts of governor-general of Liang-Chiang and imperial co
missioner in charge of all anti-Taiping operations in May 1860, whicl
gave him the formal authority and direct access to funds which he ha
sought but the court had withheld for years, symbolically coincided w
the beginning of Li Hsiu-ch'eng's last great campaigns.

Tseng's counterstrategy called for Hunan Army forces under his
own command to proceed eastward from the central Yangtze area toward Nanking in a step-by-step recovery of lost territory. Simultaneously Tso Tsung-t'ang and Li Hung-chang, his principal subordinate
took charge of clearing the provinces of Chekiang and Kiangsu respec
tively and then approaching Nanking from the east. The government
recapture of the key city of Anking, in northern Anhwei, in Septembe
1861 after a long siege and a great battle with immense casualties or
both sides, was the military turning point in the campaign from the
west. With the assistance of both foreign trained and led irregulars
(the "Ever Victorious Army" under the command first of the America
Frederick T. Ward, and later of a British officer, Charles G. Gordc
and regular British and French troops in small numbers, the city of
Shanghai was successfully defended in 1860 and 1862. Foreign aid of
this kind--including naval bombardments--also played a role in cleari
the area immediately around Shanghai and in the recapture of Ningpo
(May 1862), Soochow (December 1863), and Hangchow (March 1864).
While not without some significance, the foreign role in the suppressi
of the rebellion was quite secondary. Principal credit for the defeat

the Taipings in east China was earned by Tso Tsung-t'ang and by
Li Hung-chang's Huai Army which had emerged in 1862 as an independent force.

Li Hsiu-ch'eng's diminished troops were steadily forced back
towards Nanking. In that city conditions became increasingly desperate. Tseng Kuo-fan with the aid of the foreign consuls in Shanghai
had at last instituted an effective blockade; food was short; the Heavenly King shut himself in his palace and offered no leadership; bick-
ering and intrigues for petty power hampered the defense. Tseng
Kuo-ch'üan, the younger brother of Tseng Kuo-fan, commanded the
final assault on the rebel capital, which fell to his troops on July
19, 1864. A vast slaughter followed. Tseng Kuo-fan's report to the
throne that 100,000 rebels were killed was probably a rhetorical
exaggeration. What is certain is that none survived from the original Taiping core of God-worshippers from Kwangsi and Kwangtung.
They both resisted to the last and were systematically massacred.
Hung Hsiu-ch'üan commited suicide on June 1, 1864; he was 51 years
old. Li Hsiu-ch'eng, Hung Hsiu-ch'üan's sixteen-year-old son, and
Hung Jen-kan escaped from Nanking and briefly eluded the government
troops before they were captured and executed. The Loyal King died
on August 7, after having composed for his captors a long autobio-
graphical "confession" which is a major source for the history of the
Taiping movement. Some Taiping forces under semiindependent commanders were able to escape the pincers which Tseng Kuo-fan and his
lieutenants had so brilliantly executed. Most were annihilated in the
following year or two. The remnants joined with the Nien rebels, and
helped to keep that rebellion alive in north China until 1868.

+ The foregoing account of the main features of the rebellion, in
particular the discussion of its ideology and institutions, has already
suggested in passing some of the factors that defeated the Taiping
effort to unseat the Ch'ing dynasty. I shall return later to these
more general causes for the failure of rebellion in nineteenth-century
China. Here it may be useful to restate briefly some more immediate reasons for the Taiping defeat that seem obvious to us now, however unlikely it is that the rebels could have acted otherwise than they
did. The failure to mount a full-scale attack on Peking early in 1853,
which probably was within their capabilities, was an obvious strategic
error. Similarly, the omission of any attempt to control Shanghai and
other east China cities in the early 1850s, while the foreign govern-
ments were taking a substantially neutral position toward the parties

in China's civil war, now appears a mistake. How much the Taiping failure to support the Small Sword Society seizure of Shanghai and Ningpo in 1853 was determined by a growing ideological antipathy between the radical God-worshippers and the traditional secret societies with their Ming restorationist outlook is difficult to say. It is symbolic of the inability of the Taipings to rally all the potential anti dynastic forces under their banner.

The moral decay of some of the original leadership is hardly s unique a phenomenon as to surprise us. Its consequences were appa ently severe after the purges of 1856, but they are difficult to isolate from other more general factors affecting the outcome of the rebellio And, finally, I note that profound ignorance on the part of the Taipin leaders of the Western powers with whom it might conceivably have been possible to reach some anti-Ch'ing understanding in the period before the Treaties of Tientsin were signed. Never more than the faintest and most tenuous possibility in any case, it was undermined by attitudes of cultural arrogance on the part of the rebels that differed only minimally from those of their imperial opponents.

The Nien Rebellion

If, as I have suggested, the Taipings after 1856 entered a centrifugal quasi-warlord phase which raises doubts about treating the rebellion as a unified movement after that date, it is even more difficult to accept the idea of a single Nien rebellion. The marauding attacks by armed bands (including substantial cavalry forces) on the villages and smaller cities of north China between 1851 and 1868 which are subsumed under the heading "Nien Rebellion" arose out of circumstances of local disorder similar to those which created the Taipings. Unlike the Taipings, however, the Nien were characterize by a low level of ideological consciousness, had little or no formal political organization, did not directly administer the territories in which they operated, and did not maintain a bureaucratized professional army. In spite of these shortcomings, the Ch'ing regular army (Banner and Green Standard units) proved unable either to reassert imperial control in the countryside of Anhwei, Shantung, and Honan where the Niew were strong, or to destroy the Nien guerrilla armies. So effective in fact had the latter become that in the spring of 1865 they badly defeated a large Ch'ing army in Shantung, includin cavalry components from Manchuria and Inner Mongolia, and killed it commander, the vaunted Seng-ko-lin-ch'in. For all that, it is still difficult to distinguish the Nien from other "bandits," secret society dissidents, and armed salt smugglers who were endemic in north China in the first half of the century. Might it not be that the idea of a single, organized Nien rebellion is a reflection of exaggerated accounts of their enemies by Ch'ing officials and generals seeking to excuse or conceal their own failure to cope with widespread but largely uncoordinated rural unrest?

The term "Nien" appears to be a local expression in western Anhwei and eastern Honan meaning roughly a gang of people tied together in some form of organization. In the early 1850s it referred to local groups of armed bandits, possibly related to the White Lotus sect, who were scattered throughout the border districts of the provinces of Anhwei, Honan, Shantung, and Kiangsu. The dispersed Nien bands were able to maintain themselves against government forces in part by infiltrating and controlling the walled villages and local militia which had become widespread phenomena in north China since the suppression of the White Lotus uprising at the beginning of the nineteenth century. Two developments swelled their ranks and pushed the Nien in the direction of a more coordinated attack on the government. First, the Taiping northern expedition against Peking in 1853 passed through Huai-pei (north of the Huai river), as the territory in which they were active was called. The Taiping uprising gave the Nien both the chance, because it diverted Ch'ing forces to the south, and the inspiration to develop into an antidynastic movement. Nien bands fought with the Taiping expeditionary army in 1853, and thereafter loose ties were maintained between the two insurgent groups. The second development was the change of the course of the Yellow river in 1855 which brought disastrous flooding to much of Huai-pei and produced numerous Nien recruits from among the sorely stricken peasantry.

Between 1853 and 1856, the scattered Nien bands gradually and unevenly came together in a number of larger groups under several leaders. Although they were still poorly organized, some of the insurgent chiefs had grand pretensions as evidenced by such titles as "Son of Heaven to Found a New Nation," or "The Great Sage to Equal Heaven." Taiping influence is evident in these and other slogans and titles. In 1856, a more comprehensive but still loose alliance of the five main Nien bands was formalized under the leadership of Chang Lo-hsing, who took the title "King of Great Han Possessing the Heavenly Mandate." The Nien military forces were nominally reorganized into five large "banners," i.e., units identified by the color of their flags, each in turn divided into five smaller battalions. In practice, however, until they were driven from their Huai-pei base area after 1863, the Nien armies were not full-time professionals, but were constituted by mobilizing small groups of peasants and horses from numerous local walled villages (yü) within which Nien influence was dominant. Coordination was left to ad hoc conferences among the local and regional chieftains. Nien military success before the suppression of the Taiping rebellion enabled the government to direct new armies and new tactics against them was mainly a product of the incapacity of the Ch'ing regulars to respond to the flexible guerrilla tactics of the insurgents.

Chang Lo-hsing (d. 1863), an illiterate "bandit" from Wo-yang, Anhwei, was never more than a nominal commander-in-chief; his wri did not extent beyond the communities under his direct control. He maintained a loose affiliation with the Taipings and in 1861 accepted the Taiping title of Prince of Wo-yang. After his capture by Seng-kc lin-ch'in and execution in 1863, his second cousin, Chang Tsung-yü (d. 1868), succeeded him. Tsung-yü, similarly illiterate, led the western Nien, after the insurgent forces were split in 1866, first into Shensi and then back to Shantung where they were annihilated in 1868. Two other important Nien leaders had close ties with the Taipings. Jen Chu (d. 1867), apparently also illiterate, bore the title Prince of Lu, and cooperated closely with the forces under Lai Wenkuang (1828?-1868), an educated Kwangsi native who had joined the God-worshippers in 1850 and led the Taiping remnants to join the Nien after the fall of Nanking in 1864. With the exception of Lai, these were typical "bandit" leaders: rough men, brave fighters, not the kind to be strongly committed to an ideological struggle. Even if we take seriously Chang Lo-hsing's anti-Manchu title "King of Great Han Possessing the Heavenly Mandate," he and his fellow chiefs were at best traditional rebels in the secret society, Ming restorationist tradition. Neither the Taiping-like titles, seals, and ornaments whic seemed to fascinate the Nien commanders, nor the fact that their armies were made up of peasants temporarily mobilized into fighting co umns, are serious tokens that they had any deeper revolutionary aims Nothing at all resembling the Taiping utopian outlook was ever envisaged by the Nien. Peasant support, for example, which seems to ha been ample before 1863, was based on resistance to specific local grievances, and not on the anticipation of a new social order.

The dependence of the Nien bands on their home communities was a critical one. Consolidation of this base by gaining control of ever larger numbers of local walled communities, especially in northwest Anhwei, went on through the years 1856-1859. This was often accomplished as much by winning the support of the local militia units who dominated the walled villages as by direct conquest. Nien raids into Shantung and Honan in this period were often for the purpose of obtaining food, horses, and military supplies for their Huai-pei base. Between 1859 and 1863, the Nien forces were increasingly on the offensive and infested a large number of smaller cities in the Huai river valley. No reliable figures are available, but according to (possibly exaggerated) government estimates, the rebels in 1860 totalled 100,000 armed men and dominated an area of some 90,000 square miles.

After repeated government failures to suppress the Nien, the Manchu court in 1860, the war with England and France having been concluded, seconded its most capable general, the Mongol prince Seng-ko-lin-ch'in, to that task. His redoubtable Manchu and Mongol cavalry, reinforced by Banner troops and Green Standard battalions, was slow in getting started. In February 1863, Seng-ko-lin-ch'in inflicted a major defeat on the Nien forces in Anhwei, but decisive victory eluded him. The prince was surrounded by Nien forces under Lai Wen-kuang in May 1865 and killed. The Nien captured a large number of horses in this battle and were enabled to enlarge their already formidable cavalry. Seng-ko-lin-ch'in's failure was in part a consequence of the harshness with which he treated not just the rebel leaders who fell into his hands, but also the rank and file and the peasant communities from which they came.

The death of Seng-ko-lin-ch'in forced the court to order Tseng Kuo-fan to take command of the imperial effort against the Nien rebels. Tseng under pressure from Peking had already disbanded the largest part of his Hunan Army and had to depend initially on the reluctant cooperation of officials and gentry leaders in north China to execute his policy of combining political "pacification" of the rebel areas with military measures. Increasingly, however, Li Hung-chang on Tseng's orders deployed his Huai Army--50,000 men with strong cavalry units and some modern weapons--in the Nien areas. The Tseng-Li strategy called for depriving the Nien of their base area in Huai-pei by penetrating and reorganizing the walled communities which had supported the rebels (the same "strengthening the

walls and clearing the countryside" which had defeated the White
Lotus sixty years earlier), and gradually mopping up the Nien armed
bands. The Nien, however, still had the force to break through
Tseng's blockade in the summer and autumn of 1866. Thereafter,
deprived of their base area and assured sources of men and supplies,
the rebels split into two parts. The eastern Nien under the command
of Lai Wen-kuang and Jen Chu remained a potent mobile force which
rampaged through Shantung, Honan, and Hupei before they were finally
annihilated by Li Hung-chang, who in early 1867 had replaced Tseng
Kuo-fan as imperial commander-in-chief, in a series of bloody battles
in Shantung in November-December 1867. While the eastern Nien
were confronting Li Hung-chang's main forces, the western detachment
under Chang Tsung-yü moved into Shensi seeking to join with the Muslim insurgents in that province. This alliance proved abortive, and
Chang next led his augmented forces in the direction of Peking, coming
to within eighty miles of the captial before he was thrown back into
Shantung. There, relentlessly pursued by Li Hung-chang and Tso
Tsung-t'ang, without a stable supply base such as they had had in the
past, the last of the Nien were finally eliminated in a great slaughter
in the summer of 1868.

Miao, Muslim, and Other Rebellions

Galvanized by the increased burden of taxes to finance the war
against the Taiping forces in Kweichow and the border areas of Hunan,
Kwangsi, Yunnan, and Szechwan which they inhabited, the fragmented
revolts of the Miao minority population which were almost endemic in
the first half of the nineteenth century coalesced into a substantial
challenge to Ch'ing (and Han Chinese) control which lasted from 1855
to 1872. The Miao revolt was accompanied by secret society uprisings
in Kweichow (possibly with White Lotus connections), and intermittently
cooperated with Shih Ta-k'ai's Taiping bands which erupted into Kweichow. Given the preoccupation of the dynasty with the much greater
threat from the Taipings and Nien, little coordinated effort was made
to pacify the Miao before the fall of Nanking in 1864. Hsi Pao-t'ien
(1829-1889), one of Tseng Kuo-fan's Hunanese lieutenants, then took
command of a large contingent of the Hunan Army and other veterans
of the Taiping war which was directed against the Miao. Aided by
favorable terrain and effective guerrilla tactics, the rebellion managed
to stay alive until May 1872 when its leader, Chang Hsiu-mei, and a
number of allied secret society chieftains were at last captured and
executed.

On a larger scale than the Miao insurrection were the contemporaneous uprisings of the Muslim populations of southwest and northwest China which grew out of cultural conflict and economic discrimination. The rebellion of the Yunnan Muslims ("Panthay Rebellion") continued from 1855 to 1873, and consisted of two largely separate uprisings. The covert leader of the first was one Ma Te-hsin, a religious teacher who had made the pilgrimage to Mecca and maintained nominal loyalty to the government, while his disciple Ma Ju-lung (d. 1891) commanded the Muslim insurgents in eastern Yunnan. Ma Ju-lung's forces had considerable success, even threatening Kunming, the provincial capital, before he was induced to accept "pacification" in 1862 by the Ch'ing commander Ts'en Yü-ying (1829-1889). Ju-lung was the holder of a lower military degree, and his family apparently had a considerable military tradition. His surrender and subsequent appointment to fairly high military posts by the government is an illustration of the possibility of moving from the command of hetereodox to orthodox military formations which I shall discuss below. Tu Wen-hsiu (d. 1872), who led the rebellion in western Yunnan, was unlike Ma Ju-lung deeply committed ideologically to the cause of Muslim separatism. He has been compared to Hung Hsiu-ch'üan for the intensity of his opposition to the Manchu-Chinese dynasty and for his religious devotion to Islam. From his capital at Tali, Tu controlled all of western Yunnan as far as the Burmese border before he was captured and executed in December 1872. Ts'en's forces completed the annihilation of his followers in 1873. Yunnan suffered heavily from eighteen years of civil strife; it is estimated that of the eight million persons who lived in the province before 1855, five million perished or fled--literary exaggeration, no doubt, but the devastation was apparent to travellers even two decades later.

The Muslim revolt in the northwest provinces of Shensi and Kansu ("Tungan Rebellion") broke out in June 1862, escalating rapidly from a local riot in Shensi. Ch'ing encouragement of the formation of local militia (t'uan-lien) for defense against the Taipings had provided both the Han Chinese and Muslim communities with a military potential which could easily get out of hand where old interethnic grievances abounded. The uprising spread to Kansu, and then--much more critical for the Manchu government--into Chinese Central Asia, where the Turkic speaking Muslims in what became the province of Sinkiang in 1884 rose up against the Manchu-Chinese colonial administration. To complicate the situation further, in 1870 a Central Asian adventurer named Yakub Beg (1820-1877), who had come to Sinkiang in the early years of the revolt, made himself the head of a Muslim kingdom there which he sought to sustain by entering into relations with England and Russia. Suppression of the rebellion in the northwest eventually involved China in a diplomatic imbroglio, the long-range consequences of which are still apparent in the hostile relations between the Soviet Union and the People's Republic of China in Central Asia.

Again the tasks of suppressing the Taipings and Nien took precedence; only in 1867 was Tso Tung-t'ang put in command of the effort to pacify the Muslim northwest. Tso's preparations were careful and lengthy. The Hunan troops which he recruited, like those which defeated the Taipings, were well-trained, equipped with modern weapons, and adequately paid. Shensi was pacified by the spring of 1869, Kansu only at the end of 1873. Tso's strategy for the recovery of the rebellious areas, like that of Tseng Kuo-fan against the Taipings, called for political and economic measures to regain the support of the populace as well as for superior military force. British and Russian support for Yakub Beg delayed Tso's reconquest of Sinkiang, which was completed only in 1878. Deaths during the rebellion and the flight of refugees are said to have reduced the population of Kansu province from 15,000,000 to 1,000,000. Again, literary hyperbole; but, again, the deserted villages and ruined fields are described by contemporary observers as stretching for mile

If the Taipings, Nien, Miao, and Muslims were the most danger ous threats to the dynasty in the middle years of the nineteenth centur innumerable lesser rebellions, usually under secret society leadership complicated the dynasty's task of devising a successful response to these possibly fatal insurrections. The Small Sword Society (Hsiao-tao hui), a branch of the Triad secret society, seized Shanghai in September 1853 and held it until February 1855. Amoy was invested for six months by the same insurgent group. Triad bands were particularly active in Kwangsi and Hunan in 1854 and 1855, and controlle much of the former province for several years. Other Triads attacke Canton in 1855 and 1856 as part of a struggle with imperial forces in Kwangtung which is said to have cost several hundred thousand lives. The insurrections in Kwangtung and Kwangsi were interwoven with an intermittent but bloody communal war (1854-1857) between the Hakka linguistic minority and earlier settlers (pen-ti, or commonly "Punti") throughout the West River (Hsi-chiang) valley. In Kiangsi, Szechwan, and Kwangsi, secret society bands at times cooperated with Shih Ta-

k'ai's Taiping army (in Kwangsi, the two sometimes fought each
other as well) in joint attacks on government forces. Recent Chinese Communist historiography has discovered a hitherto neglected
large-scale insurrection in Shantung, north China, in the early 1860s
led by one Sung Ching-shih. How many more on this scale, and how
many unrecorded lesser protests against officials and landlords were
stimulated by the mounting context of armed challenge to established
state and society in these decades I am unable to say. That the cumulative blow struck the dynasty by "domestic disorder" of this scale
and scope was unprecedented during the Ch'ing seems, however, beyond question.

Yet the Ch'ing survived, "restored" its rule, and even undertook wide-ranging "reforms" in the four decades before it succumbed
to the republican revolution of 1911. If the foreign imperialist threat
could not be turned back, "domestic disorder" of the traditional kind
apparently was susceptible to control by a regime refurbished through
"self-strengthening." In contrast to the troubled years I have just
surveyed, the last decades of the nineteenth century were remarkably
free of serious internal armed rebellions. The Boxer uprising in
North China which ushered in the new century indeed posed a threat
to the dynasty before its anti-Manchu components were lopped off in
1899 and the movement, with court and official encouragement, shunted
onto a track labeled "support the Ch'ing; destroy the foreigner" (fu-
Ch'ing mieh-yang). Perhaps the virulent xenophobia of the Boxers,
like the dozens of attacks on foreign missionaries and Christian converts (chiao-an, "missionary incidents") in the last half of the nineteenth century, for some of which secret society elements were
clearly responsible, can be seen as the form into which some quan-
tity of popular discontent was transmuted, and hence as still potentially dangerous to the dynasty. The context, however, had begun
to change after the suppression of the mid-century rebellions. With
its new level of militarization, the political and social elite were now
able to suppress domestic rebellion quite efficiently. But because of
its failure to oust the foreigner, in the meanwhile elite expectations
about the dynasty itself had been perceptibly altered. The new types
of antidynastic rebellion which first appear at the turn of the cen-
tury--Sun Yat-sen's abortive efforts at Canton (1895) and Waichow
(1900), and the Tzu-li Hui uprising led by T'ang Ts'ai-chang (1900)--
although they were dependent on secret society support, at least
pointed to objectives (constitutional government, republicanism) which
remove them entirely from the universe of "domestic disorder" with
which this essay is concerned.

SOURCES OF SOCIAL DISSIDENCE

In discussing the causes of rebellion in nineteenth-century China, it is useful to distinguish three general clusters of contributory factors. I shall consider in turn: continuing or newly developed "strains" or "dislocations" in Chinese society; the ideologies which draw attention to these problems and have the capacity to generalize the discontent which they engender; and the availability or development of social institutions--organized groups of people--through which dissent can be expressed.

Social Strains

Economic Stagnation

While the Chinese economy at the beginning of the nineteenth century might be described as "underdeveloped" (in its technology and total output) in comparison not only with twentieth-century industrial society but even with Europe in the early stages of the industrial revolution, within the limits of the traditional technology available to it late-Ch'ing China was highly "developed" indeed. This maturity, in fact, was itself a major source of the social strains which nourished rebellion. In the four centuries between 1400 and 1800 (from the early Ming dynasty to mid-Ch'ing) China's population had grown from ca. 65-80 million to ca. 400-450 million, a sixfold increase. Cultivated acreage tripled in the same period, growing from ca. 425 million mou to ca. 1,200 million. Apart from the destructiveness of the late-Ming rebellions of Li Tzu-ch'eng and Chang Hsien-chung and the toll exacted by the Manchu conquest, these were centuries of relative internal tranquility. Through the development of the full potential of the available technology and its diffusion over the entire area of China proper, per capita consumption of food, clothing, housing and other necessities was maintained at a constant level in spite of population growth at twice the rate of increase of cultivated land. The level of consumption was low and it was always precarious, a hostage to flood and drought, profligate officials and wicked landlords, endemic banditry and sometimes civil war. But by opening new areas to cultivation, greatly increasing crop yields per unit of land by such means as the multiplication of double cropping (which itself served to employ the growing labor force), and to a lesser extent by introducing

47

new grain crops (corn and potatoes) from America, output per capita was sustained.

Up to a point traditional agriculture clearly had the capacity to grow within its given technology and to sustain large population increases. But only up to the point at which the supply of virgin land was exhausted and/or the potentialities of the traditional technology were exceeded by the size and complexity of the inputs required for further expansion. By 1800 the supply of usable land within China proper had been largely brought under cultivation: Szechwan and the areas in Hupei and Shensi which were depopulated by the late-Ming rebellions had not only recovered their earlier population but continued to be faced with large migrations of newcomers for whom only marginal land was available; and from early Ming onward south and southwest China and had gradually been filled up by new migrants. Central Asia, newly brought under Ch'ing domination in the eighteenth century, was underpopulated. But, apart from the hostility of indigenous non-Han populations to Chinese settlers, little of that vast territory was amenable to Chinese-type agriculture. Manchuria was the only real frontier remaining. It did benefit from substantial Chinese settlement in the nineteenth century as the Manchus abandoned their earlier effort to maintain their homeland as a non-Sinified preserve. The development of Manchuria, however, was hampered by its distance (by traditional means of transportation), the large capital inputs required, and the relative lateness of Chinese migration.

That the traditional technology, moreover, had reached a point of diminishing returns intensified the contradiction between continued population growth and a contraction in the supply of unopened land which began to be apparent in the last half of the eighteenth century. Little change in the kind or quality of farm implements had occurred over the four centuries of economic growth from 1400 to 1800, but capital inputs in the form of local water control projects--canals, dykes, dams, reservoirs, terraces--had been undertaken by the tens of thousands to facilitate the opening of new land and the remarkable extension of double cropping. By 1800, in the absence of a more advanced technology which employed steam, electricity, or the internal combustion engine to service provincial or regional needs, the marginal land still available for cultivation could not be easily or economically opened.

Thus, at the height of the Ch'ing dynasty, in the middle of the glorious reign of the Ch'ien-lung emperor, it can be said that for the first time the Chinese empire as a whole began to be faced with a fateful problem which hitherto had only made itself felt in some areas and for limited times: the inexorable pressure of a growing population on a limited supply of land. Reflections of this problem began to appear in writings of the last quarter of the eighteenth century where we find expressions of alarm at the conspicuous decline in the level of consumption as compared with the beginning of the century. Hung Liang-chi (1746-1809), for example, noted though obviously with little empirical precision that "population has increased . . . at least twenty times over what it was one hundred and some tens of years ago . . . so that there is a shortage of homes and fields but a surplus of people." In Hung's view, superficially similar to that of his contemporary, Thomas Malthus, the only effective controls on population growth were "flood, drought, sickness and epidemics." The ruler could only exhort his people to open new lands, prohibit extravagant living, assess his taxes equitably, and offer relief when it was needed. Hung concluded, "In sum, during a period of prolonged peace Heaven and Earth cannot but propagate the human race, but the resources which Heaven and Earth can make available to support man are limited. As for the government, it cannot prevent the population from multiplying during a period of prolonged peace, but the means it has to provide for the people's needs are limited."

We can conclude that nineteenth-century China saw at least a stagnating rate of economic growth, if not an absolute decline in output, while population continued to increase until the great mid-century rebellions provided a kind of Malthusian safety valve by the millions of fatalities they occasioned and through their temporary effect on the birth rate. The consequences for social dissidence were multiple: a larger quantum of economic dissatisfaction and conflict over economic issues, a diminished ability to recover from the damage of inevitable natural disaster, the increased availability of peasant recruits for bandit and rebel gangs, a general decrease in the sense of local security to which populations responded by erecting walls around their towns and villages and raising militia, and probably most important--a progressive "exhaustion" of the competence of the traditional political structure to maintain order in face of the mounting tensions resulting from too many people and too little land.

Political "Exhaustion"

Part of what I have in mind in suggesting near lethal consequences for the polity is the common assertion that the Chinese government became increasingly corrupt in the nineteenth century and that official corruption, spreading from the court to the lowest local magistrate, was the primary cause of disorder and rebellion. The nature of "corruption" in the Chinese political system (which I treat elsewhere--not in this essay) suggests that there is no reason to believe that, even given the many virtues of the Chinese polity, its incidence was unusually low. And it is reasonable to assume that this "normal" quantum of depravity among both officials and their numerous underlings was enhanced by the more precarious economic conditions of the nineteenth century, and that the spreading illegal opium trade, which was dependent upon official connivance, contributed to their debauchery. The repeated references to corruption by contemporary Chinese writers are understandable in view of the Confucian proclivity to attribute calamities to moral causes. But some at least of the emphasis by historians on increased corruption as the cause of the great mid-century rebellions originates elsewhere. One of the more baneful products of the "treaty system" whose origin were traced in previous chapters was what we might call the "treaty port mentality" or the "old China hand outlook." Its characteristic disparagement was manifest in the foreign press in the treaty ports after mid-century and filled the increasing number of first-hand accounts of the Middle Kingdom prepared for readers at home. The condescension of the proconsul, merchant, and missionary toward Chinese political institutions and administratives procedures was roote in part in ignorance of the theory and practice of a remarkable political system and in part in an implicit racism. "Mandarin" ways-- this was the usual opprobious term--were sometimes inexplicable and certainly inefficient from the point of view of the aggressive foreigne who had "opened" China with opium, gunboats, and Bibles. Their inability to realize quickly the financial and ecclesiastical fruits prom ised by their easy victories in the wars of 1840-1842 and 1858-1860 was attributed to the deceit, corruption, and self-seeking of Chinese officialdom. This view colored not only the influential early scholarl treatments of late-Ch'ing China by Western writers but also the outlook of Chinese scholars of the Republican era whose immediate heritage was the anti-Manchu revolution of 1911.

Rather than a simple increase in corruption flowing from weak emperors and reactionary officials--though there was that too--the more fundamental fact was that, like the traditional economy, the Ch'ing political system too had reached a point of diminishing returns in the nineteenth century. Neither the inherited civil nor military institutions were capable of constraining the new higher level of local disorder which became almost endemic after the turn of the century. This incapacity in turn incited the organization of nonofficial attempts to maintain local order which, by their ambiguous relationship to the formal polity, only contributed further to the contraction of official competence.

This development is clearest in the case of the Ch'ing military structure. The Eight Banners, the core of Manchu military power in the early years of the dynasty and still firmly under the control of the court and royal family, had largely declined as an effective military force by the Yung-cheng period (1723-1735). For both internal control and its Central Asian campaigns the dynasty was increasingly dependent upon the larger, ethnically Chinese, Army of the Green Standard. This "regular army" was normally posted in small units throughout the provinces. The troops were in a sense "territorials," but their officers were part of a sharply defined bureaucratic hierarchy whose apex was in Peking. Military emergencies were met by assembling provincial battalions into larger armies under the command of generals deputed by the central government. While governors-general and governors had ultimate responsibility for military as well as civil affairs in their jurisdictions and held nominal concurrent appointments in the Board of War, the normal practice of rotating these officials from post to post after relatively short terms, and the requirement that the Board of War approve the appointment and dismissal of military officers, meant that the highest provincial officials were divorced from the actual management of troops. Lower provincial officials, prefects, and magistrates were also accountable for all events in their jurisdictions, but lacked even the nominal military authority of the governors-general and governors.

These cumbersome arrangements probably worked well to prevent any effective provincial challenge to Ch'ing central authority, which was a basic reason for their original implementation. But they were grossly inefficient in dealing with the endemic local disorder of the nineteenth century out of which larger rebellion could grow. Local prefects and magistrates lacked the military facilities to nip bandit gangs, secret society bands, and armed smugglers in the bud. The assembly and despatch of fragmented garrison forces not only took time, but was often resented by the local populace and officials who were pressed by the regular army officers to provide funds in addition to statutory allowances and laborers to transport baggage and dig fortifications. No wonder that "deals" with rebels were often made, that the immediate effort of many local officials should have been to chase bandits and rebels from their jurisdictions as quickly as possible rather than to fight them, that more and more frequently it was expedient to ignore local disorder rather than to be blamed by one's superiors for not suppressing it. This was corruption of a kind, certainly demoralization at the critical local political level which could have ominous consequences, but it was less a matter of personal moral failure than a sympton of major strain within the political system as a whole.

Administrative decay, more akin to what is normally called corruption but involving too a genuine "exhaustion" of the organizational and technical competence of the Ch'ing officials, may also be illustrated by the Yellow River Administration. This agency was charged with controlling the flooding of that river in order that the strategic Grand Canal which brought grain shipments to Peking could operate without interruption. Given the continuous silting which progressively raised the river bed, it was a matter of considerable technical difficulty to maintain the dikes and carry out the dredging. It was also a costly undertaking--even without a "rake-off" by greedy officials. What apparently happened in the late eighteenth and early nineteenth centuries is that the staff of the Administration grew to an enormous size as a consequence of two mutual reinforcing factors: the increased technical difficulty of controlling a river whose flood problems were cumulative and required progressively larger appropriations for dredging and the like; and the concommitant greater opportunity for private benefit if larger public funds were made available. The officials in charge were not technically competent to deal with the hydrological complexities they faced. Their numbers grew because more flood control work had to be supervised, and there were unique opportunities for "squeeze"--one contemporary writer suggests that officials built dikes badly and then neglected them so that they would "rot faster, decay faster, and be carried away faster, thereby justifying the request for more appropriations." The larger numbers of redundant bureaucrats reduced even the low prior level of efficiency, and in 1855 catastrophe came. As we have seen, in that year the Yellow river burst its dikes in Honan, left its bed, and changed its course with disastrous flooding which not only cut the Grand Canal but, for our purposes much more important, also drove thousands of stricken peasants in Huai-pei into the ranks of the Nien rebels.

"Militarization" of Society

The economic and political strains which I have just discussed, in addition to their more direct effects, gave rise to widespread local efforts to resist the spread of social disorder. In response to a growing threat to security, and beginning in the border regions of north China where the White Lotus rebellion had raged, local communities acted to protect themselves by erecting walls and re-cruiting militia. The famous walled villages (yü) in Anhwei, Honan, and Shantung which became the nuclei of Nien rebel power in the 1850s and 1860s had in many cases been fortified by their inhabitants for protection against local bandits before they were conquered by the Nien. Local fortifications of this kind were descended from the "strengthen the walls and clear the countryside" tactic which contri-buted to the suppression of the White Lotus rebellion. As the Nien showed, however, fortified points of this type might by utilized by heterodox rebellious forces as well as by troops under the command of orthodox officials.

The spread of local militia units throughout China by mid-century, involving as it did the arming of ever larger numbers of men, was characterized by a similar ambiguity with respect to the maintenance of local order. It was not always simple to distinguish between local populations arming for self-defense and secret society armed bands with other ultimate motives. If Hakka and Punti villages armed them-selves to prosecute bloody communal feuds, there was a danger that the resulting violence could be directed against the state. And even when the militia was recruited and led by orthodox local gentry, what was to guarantee that their interests and that of the dynasty would always coincide?

Military power in China, before the introduction of modern weapons, was "labor intensive." It did not depend, that is, upon the control of a complex modern armaments industry and sophisti-cated logistics. Local or regional challengers to central authority could match the military power that Peking might direct against them by controlling sufficient population and food resources. Leader-ship capacity, almost exclusively the province of the local elite, of course was critical, and the dynasty's response to rebellion conse-quently depended greatly upon its ability to mobilize that leadership under its banner. When, however, with imperial endorsement or without, the local elite organized militia units, this too had ambiguous consequences for local order. Not only was gentry power potentially enhanced at the expense of the state, but under the guise of suppressing bandits the militia might in practice be turned against the poor and dispossessed in local society whose grievance stemmed in part from increased taxes or other imposts collected by the elite, with official sanction, for the alleged purpose of defraying militia costs. This gentry "squeeze" in turn could be a source of further social dissidence.

What Philip Kuhn has brilliantly described as the progressive "militarization" of the nineteenth-century Chinese society, although it was in part a response to existing economic and political strains, could thus itself induce secondary strains potentially as dangerous as the primary contradictions.

Foreign Impact

Karl Marx, writing in the <u>New York Daily Tribune</u> of June 14, 1853, ascribed the origins of the Taiping rebellion to the displacement of handicraft spinning and weaving by the competition of imported English cotton goods: "In China the spinners and weavers have suffered greatly under this foreign competition, and the community has become unsettled in proportion. " Marx's picture of China in the 1850s, before imported cotton goods had any significant effect, appears to be a transposition to China of perhaps an equally implausible analysis of contemporary Indian conditions. (From the 1870s, textile imports did have important consequences for the Chinese economy.) It has, nevertheless, become a <u>locus classicus</u> for the view, often repeated in recent Chinese historiography, that the mid-century rebellions were the product of imperialist economic exploitation in concert with Manchu "feudal" oppression. It does not appear that foreign impact contributed in any way to the White Lotus or other outbreaks early in the century, and cotton imports were not yet significant in the time of the Taipings and Nien. In a number of other important ways, however, the newly arrived foreigner and his trade and evangelism were responsible for dislocations in Chinese society which aggravated the more traditional strains already recounted.

The opium trade, which expanded after the Treaty of Nanking, was conducted in circumstances rife with smuggling and piracy which inspired or amplified local disorder. When British naval vessels undertook to suppress troublesome pirates on the Kwangtung coast in 1849, the pirate gangs were forced to move inland up the West

River into Kwangsi province, where they added to the already bur-
geoning lawlessness. Some joined with the Taipings and played a
key role in providing and directing the flotillas which carried the
rebels to the Yangtze and down its course to Nanking. Additional
manpower to swell the rebellion was furnished by unemployed transport workers who, prior to the development of Shanghai as the major
entrepot for tea and silk exports, had carried these goods in their
boats and on their backs over the Cheling and Meiling passes in the
Nan Ling mountains on the long route to Canton.

To these consequences of trade with the foreigner should be
added the loss of prestige to the dynasty resulting from its defeat
in the Opium War, especially in the south which had held out longest
against the Manchu conquest. The principal target of Cantonese
xenophobia--or proto-nationalism?--was still the foreigner. It was
to repel him that the villagers' local militia led by patriotic gentry
had assembled at San-yuan-li in 1841; and the officials' delay in
opening Canton city to foreign residence in the 1840s on the grounds
that popular anti-foreign sentiment was uncontrollable was not entirely a pretext. Militarization in the Canton area was one instance of
a general response to local disorder which we have noted, in this
case the disorder of a foreign threat to the city. The dispersal of
the San-yuan-li militia by the Ch'ing government, however, symbolically planted the first seeds of a resentment against Manchu appease-
ment of the foreigner which decades later were to bear bitter fruit.
Rebellion against the dynasty because it was incapable of defending
the Chinese nation against the incursions of foreign imperialism was
not yet a burning cause in the mid-nineteenth century. When it
became the central issue--potentially in the case of the Boxers,
actually for Sun Yat-sen and the republican revolutionary movement
--rebellion in Chinese society entered a new phase which extends
beyond the limits of this essay.

One final, and important but possibly overemphasized, contri-
bution of the West to rebellion in nineteenth-century China was the
version of Protestant Christianity which Hung Hsiu-ch'üan and Feng
Yün-shan taught to their Hakka followers on Mt. Thistle. Without
the larger context of social strain, which made rebellion possible,
there would have been little to differentiate Hung's new sect from
other heterodox religious associations.

The Ideologies of Rebellion

Economic deprivation, political corruption and repression, and socially retrogressive actions by the political and social elite are by themselves not enough to arouse the lower classes, those who are deprived or exploited, to attempt to overthrow the existing social system. Some forms of rebellion possibly, and certainly social protest at the lower end of the hierarchy of dissidence, can occur without a comprehensive revolutionary ideology. But genuine revolutionary attempts, and above all successful revolutions, require the mediation of ideologies which legitimize dissent and the desire for comprehensive change, and successfully subvert the legitimacy of the political and social order under attack.

"Ideology" is a protean term, with possibly as many meanings as there are users. What I have in mind are not the ultimate and often implicit values of a society which, for the very reason that they are immanent, abstract, and intrinsically untestable, are relatively invulnerable to direct attack. In the case of "Confucian" China it is difficult to imagine a successful frontal challenge to the central idea that a "harmony" exists both in nature, and in human society which is an integral part of the natural universe; to the concept that nature and society consist of an orderly hierarchy of interrelated parts and forces, all essential for the total process; to the view that change, in the form of either polar oscillation or cyclical movement, is integral to the process; or to the belief that inherent in the universe is a principle of goodness. Such fundamental beliefs are not only self-validating or self-refuting, but also permit so wide a variety of social practice that only in the very long run are they assailable.

Ideology, as I am using it here, operates at a more practical level to perform two critical tasks for a social system. It attempts to show that there is a rational connection between the specific institutional arrangements it proposes and the basic values it holds that these arrangements will in practice realize; this is the realm of social theory. Secondly, ideology attempts to persuade members of society to adopt and support the political and social arrangements it has justified; this is the domain of propaganda, argumentation, and education. Ideology in these two aspects overlaps in function although not in origin with the Marxian idea of an ideological "superstructure" which arises out of underlying social relations and permeates the political, cultural, and educational institutions of society. It provides a kind of cultural integuement which protects the actual distribution of power and wealth from both direct apprehension by those who are ruled and from frontal attack. The key to the stability of an existing social system is the ability of the political and social elite, the ruling class, to convince the nonelite, the lower classes, that the former's interests are those of society at large, that the ruling elite is the defender of common values and stands for a natural and proper social order the benefits of which accrue to the ruled as well. For a revolution to be successful this protective ideological integuement must first be shattered by a counterideology; only then can the dissatisfactions resulting from economic and political strains be mobilized against the status quo. Hence the necessity that the legitimacy of "Confucianism" as a political theory and as the substance of politics, education, high culture, and interpersonal relations be undermined. Ultimately, successful destruction of the dominant ideology might lead not only to the overthrow of the Confucian political and social system, but also to radical changes in the basic values of Chinese society.

To what extent did rebellion in nineteenth-century China present so sweeping a challenge to the Ch'ing dynasty? In answering this question, we should look both for challenges to the dominant state ideology, and for the proffer of credible alternatives. With one possible partial exception which I have treated at length above, i.e., the Taiping rebellion, the ideologies of the rebellions being considered in this essay fell short of being "revolutionary." It is possible to distinguish religious (magico-religious and millenarian), political "restorationist," populist, and ethnocentric-xenophobic themes in nineteenth-century rebel ideologies. In practice of course each insurrection was a palimpsest combining two or three of these themes; for expository convenience, I shall treat them separately.

Almost without exception the rebellions of the Ch'ing professed some religious tenets. These might be as relatively uncomplicated as the early nineteenth-century resurgence of Islam among the Muslim population of Chinese Turkestan, which fed on Muslim-Manchu religious differences and contributed to the rebellions in Yunnan and the northwest. Though Islam was potentially revolutionary in the Ch'ing Confucian context, in practice Turkestan was marginal to the Ch'ing state system, and the Muslim rebellions were "reformist" movements directed preponderantly at specific abuses by Manchu officials and Han Chinese settlers.

The religious elements in the White Lotus rebellion of 1796-
1804 were more complex, and recapitulated all of the sectarian beliefs which over the centuries had been added to an underlying local
polytheism: the magical practices of popular Taoism, the millenarian
ism of Maitreya Buddhism, Manichean struggle of the Kingdom of
Light and the Kingdom of Darkness, and the Confucian ethical system.
The rebels closely identified their political cause with a divine mission of universal salvation, but their political cause was the restoration of the Ming dynasty not a basic rearrangement of the social
order.   At best the egalitarian content of White Lotus millenarian
Buddhism was vague; it offered no real alternative to the state and
society of the Ch'ing dynasty.

As we shall see, the endemic secret societies differed widely
in the degree of their commitment to specifically religious goals;
for most of them, however, religion--Buddhist and Taoist accretions
to local spirit beliefs and medium cults--provided an important inte-
grative factor.   Their secret and elaborate initiation rites and rituals
served to tie together diverse individual interests and to give their
political opposition emotional support in the form of the sanction of
the gods.   But, like the White Lotus, although their religious ideology might seem to be radically opposed to imperial Confucianism,
these magico-religious elements were not entirely absent from the
ideology of emperors and officials, and the basic aim of those sects
which were politicized was restorationist--to replace the Ch'ing
with an ethnic Chinese dynasty--rather than social revolutionary.

Rebel populist slogans attacking official corruption, inequitable
taxes, and landlord exactions, and offering programs not only for
dynastic change but also for the curtailment of the economic and
legal privileges of the ruling class have received considerable attention by historians in the People's Republic of China.   Are these not
evidence of a revolutionary ideology? I think not. The evidence
does suggest the existence of substantial peasant unrest arising from
exploitation and economic deprivation--revolts of the despairing--
but the ideological response thereto did not stem directly from the
exploited.   It seems rather to have been a combination of 1) an attack
by the rebel leadership--not usually simple peasants--on official and
landlord deviations from the traditional Confucian norms of benevo-
lence toward the peasantry and their protection from exploitation by
the elite (cf. Mencius); 2) opposition to heavy state exactions on the
commercial (including smuggling) or real estate interests of alienated
members of the lower elite; and 3) effective propaganda by rebel

chieftains seeking to augment the size of their forces. Rather than being revolutionary attacks on the protective integuement, these populist slogans and programs were often the products of shared basic social values. The rebels--often peasants--and their leaders were, in other words, conscious of their own exploitation, but they lacked an awareness that their personal miseries were embedded in the workings of an entire social system. Chinese "Jacqueries," one might say.

There is also some support for this view in the reluctance of rebel leaders to break finally with the dynasty (symbolized by a claim to the Mandate of Heaven and the assumption of an imperial title) unless circumstances left no other recourse. Chang Lo-hsing, the chief Nien leader, formally took such steps only in 1855 and 1856, although he had been in rebellion since at least 1852. We have here a Chinese version of Eric Hobsbawm's "populist legitimism": the immediate objects of rebel discontent were the corrupt officials who had misled the ruler. As long as the emperor retained some residue of the Mandate, i.e., unless he has produced or tolerated more than the expected measure of poverty, injustice, and death, the possibility of compromise was ideologically possible. Hence the numerous instances in the Ch'ing annals of "pacification" of rebels, who were then given modest sinecures or even employed against their erstwhile fellows. Among those of some notoriety: the Muslim leader Ma Ju-lung, the Nien leaders Miao P'ei-lin, Li Chao-shou, and Chang Lo-hsing (before his imperial pretensions), and the secret society leader Sung Ching-shih. Confucian orthodoxy was not the total monopoly of the rulers, and conversely rebel ideology was not invariably heterodox.

The restorationist goals of the politicalized secret societies inevitably expressed themselves in some measure of anti-Manchu racialist propaganda. Expulsion of the "barbarian" as a mobilizing theme had had considerable appeal from the Mongol conquest onward, and in the early Ch'ing it was still a powerful slogan. By the nineteenth century, however, its glitter was somewhat dulled as the Manchu conquerors themselves had become sinified and the Chinese upper classes had been absorbed into a political and social system the benefits of which they shared with the originally alien conquerors. The scurrilous Taiping references to the "stinking odor" of the "Manchu demons," for example, in a proclamation of June 1853, made no impact on the local elite who were mobilizing militia to defend both the dynasty and Sino-Manchu society.

Antiforeignism of a different kind was expressed in the multitude of anti-Christain incidents which appeared with apparently increasing frequency after mid-century. Attacks on missionaries and Chinese converts were typically inspired or led by members of the local elite, but on other occasions--for example, the conflict at "Pear Garden Village," Kuan-hsien, Shantung, in 1887, or the "Vegetarian Society" attack on Protestant missionaries near Ku-t'ien city, Fukien, in 1895--the chiao-an were the outgrowth of rivalry between Christain converts and local secret societies. The ambiguity of local elite relations with secret societies will be noted presently. For present purposes, these cases may be taken as foreshadowing the virulent xenophobia of the Boxer uprising, which combined the slogan of "support the Ch'ing and exterminate the foreigners" with elaborate magico-religious practices which purportedly gave them immunity from the foreigners' bullets. The Boxers, however, as I have already stated, were only potentially antidynastic. The ideology of rebellion in twentieth-century China would take on new forms, some genuinely revolutionary.

Rebel Groups

Social strains and rebel ideologies expressed themselves through the insurrectionary acts of both existing and newly-developed collectivities, groups of persons perhaps originally bound together by other impulses, but now caught up in the flood tide of social disorder in late-Ch'ing China. The taxonomy of rural Chinese society, below the level of the hsien city which was for many purposes as far as the for mal writ of the imperial government extended, is blurred. The lines between collectivities were faint, and the groups I shall describe ofter overlapped or could be transformed from one into another. As a star however, we can roughly distinguish the following as meriting some attention: religious, ethnic, and linguistic minorities, lineage organizations, militia, heretical sects, secret societies, and bandits.

Religious, Ethnic, and Linguistic Minorities

In the present context, actual participation in insurrection, the most important of these minorities were the Muslim correligionists in western China and Central Asia, the Miao tribes in the mountainous areas of the southwest, and the Hakka. Two separate components should be differentiated among the Muslim communities who rose in revolt: the Turkic-speaking (predominantly Uighur) populations of Chinese Turkestan, who were ethnically quite distinct from the Chinese and had only been incorporated into the Manchu empire by the great conquests of the eighteenth century; and the "Chinese Muslims" (Hui) who were concentrated in the southwestern province of Yunnan and in Shensi and Kansu in the northwest. While the Hui population had probably originally been migrants from Central Asia, through centuries of intermarriage they had shed their racial and much of their cultural identity, retaining only the Muslim religion and associated practices to differentiate them from their Han Chinese neighbors. In spite of their having adopted the Chinese language, dress, and customs, the Hui were subject to economic and political discrimination which could, under the banner of militant religious revival, lead to rebellion. The uprising of this oppressed religious minority in Shensi and Kansu which began in 1862, and the preoccupation of the Ch'ing government with the Taiping, Nien, and Miao rebellions, provided an opportunity for the Uighur Muslims, whom the Manchus governed harshly as a military colony, to attempt to overthrow the Ch'ing administration in Chinese Turkestan.

Unlike the Chinese Muslims, the aboriginal Miao tribes located in the mountainous areas of Kweichow, Yunnan, Hunan had been relatively little acculturated. They were continually subject to the encroachment of Han Chinese migrants, to exploitation by Shan-speaking Yi landlords and chieftains, and to official pressures to abandon their indigenous culture. The Miao rebellions, like those of the American Indian, were thus in part struggles to retain a racial and tribal identity, and in part reactions to the continued loss of their marginal farmland--much of it carved out of the sides of Kweichow mountains by assiduous labor--to Han military colonists. In spite of their mountain slope settlements (inaccessible and defended by mud or stone walls), the Miao proficiency at what we now call guerrilla warfare, and their alliances with antidynastic secret society bands, the disunited Miao tribes, often speaking mutually unintelligible dialects, could only withstand Ch'ing power while the latter was preoccupied with the Taipings and the Nien.

The Muslim religion, or tribal identity, as a basis for collective action are fairly obvious. In the case of the Hakka minority, who played a central role in the Taiping drama, the superficial distinguishing characteristic was their discrete dialect. Perhaps ten million persons in Kwangtung, Kwangsi and Fukien constituted a discernable linguistic minority, settled usually in territorially distinct communities. Other cultural differences from contiguous populations were correlated with that of language. This sense of common cultural identity was one basis of Hakka collective action, and functioned in a critical way, as we have seen, to shape and constrain the outlook of the Taiping leaders. The Hakka-Punti wars in Kwangtung and Kwangsi in 1854-1867 were evidently vendetta-like conflicts between culturally defined communities. Interwoven with cultural conflict were antagonisms based on the relatively inferior economic and political status of Hakka villages and lineages. The Hakka (k'o-chia, "guest settlers") had moved southward from north and central China into Kwangtung and Kwangsi in a series of migrations, the last of which began in the eighteenth century. When they spread from the mountainous Nan-ling area into central and lowland Kwangtung and Kwangsi, they came into conflict with the resident population (pen-ti, "Punti," "native residents"). As the more recent arrivals, the Hakka lineages were smaller and included fewer influential members of the elite; and the land available to them for cultivation was in general of poorer quality. Although they were conventionally described as "hardy," "frugal," and "brave fighter," these initial drawbacks left them at a disadvantage before the established and powerful Punti lineages whom they confronted. In Kwangsi, in particular, Hakka-Punti interlineage vendettas escalated with the Punti communities, because of their relative wealth and the influence of their gentry member being able to hire militia or to call upon the government for assistance while the Hakka turned to the secret societies--especially to the Hakka-led God-worshipping Society, a heterodox religious sect with military potential--to fight for their cause. So was formed the core of the Taiping movement.

Lineage Organizations

It is notable that many of the early Hakka adherents to the God-worshipping Society came not as individuals but with their entire lineage or village (which might in fact coincide). While one should be wary of viewing Chinese society only in terms of agnatic descent groups--the family and lineage as a closed world against the wider society--in southeastern China, and to a lesser extent in the Yangtze valley provinces, the lineage formed one important basis for social organization. Its formal contours were drawn along lines of patrilineal descent and its components defined themselves in terms of the ancestor cult, but the lineage was not merely an inflated family. It was essentially a political and local organization which, in southeastern

China, most commonly took the form of a single surname village, or a distinct territory in a village of more than one surname. Corporate landholding provided the economic basis for the cohesion of the lineage, providing at least some marginal advantages even to the poorer members by, for example, defraying the expenses of festivals and ceremonies or of village schools. For the lineage was also internally differentiated with respect to social and economic status. Within this cross-class organization the elite members exercised disproportionate power, for their own advantage, but also potentially in the interest of the collectivity as a whole.

The perhaps paradoxical conjunction of private and group welfare was imbedded in the dynamic and sometimes unstable equilibrium which operated between the more powerful lineages and the state in those areas of south and central China where the lineage was prominent. Through their elite members--who gained and retained their status in part by differential access to the assets of the lineage: employment of the corporate funds which they managed in private investments, education of their sons in lineage schools in preparation for the government examinations and the degrees and access to office which these made possible--the dominant lineages exerted substantial political influence. A poorer lineage which had few gentry members on its rolls was at an obvious disadvantage in comparison. Too harassed to demand more than his tax quotas and a semblance of order, the local magistrate in effect allowed significant quasi-governmental powers to the strong lineages, who dominated their neighbors, seized land under various ruses, settled most intralineage disputes without recourse to the magistrate, engaged in tax-farming (which both provided profit to the gentry and protected weaker households in the lineage from many of the illegal surcharges), and at times defied the government itself. When this defiance was pushed too far, however, to the state remained the ultimate sanction of excluding the lineage sons from the periodical examinations, thus depriving the lineage of the men with degrees, rank, or office who were an essential foundation of its power.

Apart from the Hakka lineages who joined the Taipings, there were few significant defections from the Ch'ing dynasty by substantial Han Chinese lineages per se during the troubled nineteenth century. There is some evidence of lineage lines being one basis for the organization of separate Nien bands in the early stages of that rebellion, but this matter has not really been studied. Interlineage conflict, with ethnic overtones as in the case of the Hakka-Punti clashes and between culturally identical--even agnatically related--groups, was however a continued source of disorder in southeastern China. Disorder breeds further disorder; the consequences of lineage vendettas were an enhanced militarization of society which only deepened the prevailing sense of insecurity. If normally lineages as corporate units were not insurrectionary actors, they at times had ambiguous relationships with other types of organizations which potentially were, and poorer members of the group might become very rebellious indeed.

Militia

The modern Chinese terms min-ping (literally: "people-soldier") or min-chün ("people army"), which translate as "militia," convey quite succinctly the distinction between this type of military organization and the professional soldier. The members of a militia, although sometimes mobilized for full-time service, retain civilian roles to which they normally expect to return; they are not wholly severed from their local communities and civilian occupations, to be totally absorbed into a standing army. Within this protean formula, there were many kinds of militia units in nineteenth-century China, which differed not so much in their armaments as in their sponsorship and control, and in the degree to which they were separated from the institutions of civilian society (their "level of militarization," as Philip Kuhn calls it).

A lineage, for example, of the kind just described, might recruit a militia, filling the ranks with its more improverished members under the leadership of the lineage elite, and marshalling its corporate wealth for the purpose of local defense. In times of endemic local disorder, such as the interlineage vendettas noted earlier, its military potential as much as anything else could be decisive for a lineage's fate. Military power, too, was the means by which the dominant lineages enforced their dominion, and in the process diluted their own intralineage class differences by the collective exploitation of poorer neighboring lineages.

Local militia units organized by loyal lineages or militia confederations led by the "upright gentry" (cheng-shen) of larger multilineage communities (marketing communities, for example), while potentially they might dilute and even challenge the dynastic military forces which ultimately secured the Ch'ing political system, could be controlled or

at least regularized by the imperial state. What in fact was often
an expression of the power of local society and an enhancement of
what I have elsewhere called "Level II" of the political system, could
be assimilated to a long tradition of state-sponsored militia institutions.
The t'uan-lien ("grouping and drilling") system of the late-Ch'ing period,
a generic term under which most of the orthodox militia of the kind just
described were subsumed, accomplished precisely this accommodation of
the interests of centralized state and local society. It did so by giving
official sanction to and asserting some degree of official control over
military forces which had been initiated by the local elite and which
reflected the distribution of local power. The t'uan-lien became in
fact the foundation upon which were erected the larger, regional gentry-
led armies (like Tseng Kuo-fan's Hunan Army and Li Hung-chang's Huai
Army) which rescued the dynasty from the Taipings and Nien.

Somewhat schematically, the stages of increasing militarization
were as follows. As a genuine nonprofessional militia, the t'uan-lien
could not normally be employed effectively away from its local village.
For sustained operations more permanent forces of mercenaries were
recruited by Ch'ing civil and military officials or by the local elite.
Some of the recruits had had military training and experience in a
local militia unit. These yung units (the generic term for irregular,
mobile loyalist forces) in turn provided the basis for the organization
of authentic professional armies--indoctrinated, well-armed, reasonably
paid, and commanded with a unified strategy--by Tseng Kuo-fan and
others. (The precedent for a three-level organization of part-time
village militia, full-time guerrilla units, and regular army by the Chinese Communists in the 1930s and 1940s might be noted.)

Militia, however, were not all government-sponsored or led by
"upright gentry. " Miao P'ei-lin, as an example, began his career as
a sheng-yuan, organized an effective militia against the Nien and received high provincial posts from the Ch'ing government for his ser-
vices. He maintained on and off relations with the Nien, and was
killed in 1863 after once again transferring his forces to the rebel
cause. Other instances of "intransigent gentry" (lieh-shen) who, vol-
untarily or no, sided with the Taipings appear in the record.

In troubled times village militias were also organized by nonelite leaders, if not actually by lower class persons. Although in the
mid-nineteenth century, the gentry were still overwhelmingly rural
rather than urban--that is, there was not yet that extraordinary con-

centration of the educated and influential in the cities of eastern China which had such important consequences in the mid-twentieth century--there were local communities without gentry. The self-defense forces in these villages were potentially less firmly tied to the imperial state than were gentry-led units; in fact or in anticipation, they were often described by officials as "bogus militia" or "bandit militia." Militia units of this kind in Shantung in the 1860s and 1890s are recorded as giving as much trouble to the local government as they did to bandits. They became sometimes the foci of local resistance to taxes; in Honan for example, in the 1850s this took the form of the union of several villages whose joint forces threatened the local magistrate. The Long Spear Society (Ch'ang-ch'iang hui) in Shantung and Honan, which eventually cooperated with the Nien, originated in nonelite village militias enlisted for bandit control. Even within gentry-led militia the actual training and command of the troops were not necessarily undertaken by the nominal commanders. The subalterns employed for these tasks may have acquired their martial skills as members of secret societies or bands of smugglers. Their ties with the "underworld" continued, and in suitable circumstances--a sharpening of class tensions-- part of the militia unit could be transformed into a "bandit" gang.

The insurrectionary potential in nineteenth-century society was compounded by the possibility that illegal and heterodox organizations could themselves organize militia units (perhaps raising funds openly in the name of local defense), or, more important, furnish the basis for a competing hierarchy of militarization parallel to the orthodox hierarchy which began with the t'uan-lien and reached to the regional army.

Heretical Sects, Secret Societies, and Bandits

The Ch'ing legal code (Ta-Ch'ing lü-li) includes the following two provisions (in the language of G.T. Staunton's translation, Ta Tsing Leu Lee, London, 1810, pp. 175, 546):

Magicians, who raise evil spirits by means of magical books and dire imprecations, leaders of corrupt and impious sects, and members of all superstitious associations in general, whether denominating themselves as Mi-le-fo, or Pe-lien-kiao, or in any other manner distinguished, all of them offend against the laws, by their wicked and diabolical doctrines and practices . . . the principal in the commission of such offenses shall be

strangled, after remaining in prison the usual period,
and the accessaries shall severally receive 100 blows,
and be perpetually banished to the distance of 3000 lee.

All persons who, without being related or connected by
intermarriage establish a brotherhood or other association
among themselves, by the ceremonial of tasting blood, and
burning incense, shall be guilty of an intent to commit the
crime of rebellion. . . . All those vagabonds and disor-
derly persons who have been known to assemble together,
and to commit robberies, and other acts of violence, under
the particular designation of "Tien-tee-whee," or "The
Association of Heaven and Earth," shall, immediately after
seizure and conviction, suffer death by being beheaded.

These passages discerningly distinguish the two extreme "ideal types"
in a continuum of heterodox, "underworld" organizations which actually
or potentially defied the power of the imperial state: the heretical
sect and the secret society. As I have already noted, religious practices contributed to the integration even of the political societies, so
that many illegal associations actually existed somewhere between the
two ideal types. Government persecution, moreover, could force a
political society to disguise its enterprises behind the cover of more
or less tolerated religious activities, or a religious sect to rebel
against unbearable repression.

By licensing and regulating temples, monasteries, and Buddhist
and Taoist priests, the Ch'ing state was able to assert administrative
control over the mainstreams of the two great historical religions which
had competed with Confucian orthodoxy over the centuries. This was in
effect to give them a kind of tolerance. The waters of popular religious
practice could not, however, be so easily dammed, and unregulated heretical sects proliferated outside of the administrative routines. Like
the White Lotus religion which I described earlier, these were usually
syncretic sects which were closely adapted to local folk beliefs or by
their rituals offered an emotional sustenance which the mainstream did
not. It was not their theological heresies so much as the fact that
they were congregations of largely lower class believers outside of
official control which inspired the Ch'ing government to attempt their
suppression. The Manchu experience, as the reference to "Pe-lien-
kiao" (i. e., the White Lotus Society) in the first passage quoted above
indicates, was that some at least of the unregulated sects could be

turned to antidynastic political ends. As an eighteenth-century imperial decree denouncing the sects put it: "Worst of all, rebellious and
subversive individuals and heretical miscreants glide in among them,
establish parties and form leagues by taking membership oaths. . . .
[The misled people] form connections with rebellious parties, thus
violating the principles of government and transgressing the laws of
the empire." (quoted in C.K. Yang, Religion in Chinese Society, Berk
ley: University of California Press, 1961, p. 195, additions in origin

In practice the antiheresy law could be only sporadically enforced; many of the sects were in fact small and harmless and were
tolerated by the local populace and officials. Others, however, perhaps in response to official persecution, turned to politically threatening acts, and in the ensuing military confrontation grew to such
proportions that they indeed threatened the empire. The God-worshipping Society in Kwangsi, out of which swelled the Taiping rebellion, was one of the latter.

In the conventional history of Chinese secret societies, the Whit
Lotus Society (Pai-lien-chiao) is described as one of the two great divisions into which these illegal associations were organized. The Wh
Lotus and its branches (such as the Eight Trigrams Society [Pa-kua
chiao] and the Small Sword Society [Hsiao-tao hui]) are said to have
been dominant in north China, while in the south most of the secret
societies were affiliated with the Heaven and Earth Society (T'ien-ti
hui) which was also known as the Hung League (Hung-men) or the
Triads (San-ho hui or San-tien hui). As they were secret societies,
very little beyond legend is known about their remote origins. The
White Lotus, as religious sect or rebellious association, appears on
and off in the historical record from the twelfth century. The Triads
are said to have been organized by Buddhist monks in Fukien in the
seventeenth century, and dedicated to overthrow the Ch'ing and restor
the Ming dynasty.

In their day-to-day activities the secret societies were more
commonplace and quiescent, if an equivalent of the modern day underworld of racketeering and petty violence may be so described. For
those initiated into its esoteric rituals and passwords the association
provided a promise of mutual help and protection which undoubtedly
made it attractive to the less privileged in society who benefitted leas
from alternative foci of social organization. The secret society may
in fact have functioned as a quasi-kinship organization for the lower

classes whose family units were weakest and who profited little from lineage membership. To enter into the Triad Society, we may see from the initiation ritual, was symbolically to enter a new extended family, to join as a brother with previously unrelated men. Presumably the bulk of secret society membership came from the rural poor, but also included were persons from an intermediate stratum, between the traditional political and social elite and the lao-pai-hsing, the common people, whose role has been little studied. Itinerant merchants, jobless lower-degree holders, or disappointed aspirants, smugglers, monks and priests of a sort, disbanded military officers, yamen clerks, and the like--often literate as the peasant was not, enterprising but socially unstable--seem to have provided much of secret society leadership. In social composition, the societies were similar to some of the local militia I have described, and to the heretical sects as well. Transmutation from one posture to another, as the circumstances demanded, could be accomplished with only minor inconvenience.

The leadership layer was, I believe, the possible source of political ambiguity. While probably very few "upright gentry" adhered to secret societies, equivocal persons of the kind I have just listed had ties with both the elite and the lower classes, and at times did not scruple about playing one against the other for their own gain. To give one example: the Shanghai taotai, Wu Chien-chang, in 1853 attempted the coopt of the Small Sword Society by inducing (or permitting?) its leaders to organize militia units to defend that city against the Taipings; he even employed Small Sword adherents as part of his personal guard. Not long afterwards his militia joined fellow secret society members from outside of the city to seize Shanghai and control it for seventeen months, from June 1853 to February 1855. Or: if the usual victims of secret society rackets and extortions were the quintessential enemies of the poor, they were often the lao-pai-hsing too. The Triads and others were available, as it were, for rebellion, and could be pushed in that direction by official repression or heightened social strains, but ideologically they could be flexible, opportunist we might say.

In north China, at the time of the great rebellions, there was wide variation in the degree to which secret societies were committed to the anti-Manchu cause. On the left, so to speak, the White Lotus groups cooperated actively with the Nien. The related Eight Trigrams Society was slower to adopt this belligerency, but eventually joined the rebels. On the right stood the politically vague Ch'ing-men (apparently

an eighteenth-century offshoot of the Triads) which was more preoccupied with petty robberies, extortions, and assorted rackets--fore-
shadowing its twentieth-century incarnation as the Ch'ing-pang, the
"Green Gang," notorious in the underworld of Shanghai--than with
anti-dynastic shibboleths. The Triads in central and south China,
because the social strains I have discussed were apparently more
acute there, were more universally anti-dynastic as their mounting
activities in Kwangtung, Kweichow, Hunan, and Hupei demonstrated.

I have already suggested that in relatively normal times the
secret society unit (t'ang, "lodge" or "hall") was closely tied to the
local community from which it grew. Mutual aid, petty outlawry,
sometimes the expression of lower class resistance to heavy taxes,
these rather than rebellion were its staple activities. Secret society
infiltration or organization of militia, may, for example, be seen as
parallel to and sometimes interchangeable with the orthodox militia
enterprises which went under the general name of t'uan-lien, and
which also were localized institutions.

An intensification of social strain, however, might see some
armed men from this local reservoir in which, as it were, they had
received their military basic training, join with relatively permanent
brotherhoods of outlaws or bandits (often called tsei) who had been
thrown up in the unsettled circumstances of the mid-nineteenth century. These bandit gangs were recruited from porters and boatmen
made destitute by the shift of trade from Canton to Shanghai after
1842 and by the Taiping disruption of grain traffic on the Grand Canal
in 1853, from mercenaries demobilized after the Opium War, from
landless peasants excreted by their villages, from opium smugglers
and the pirates whom the British navy forced inland in the 1840s--
that is, from persons already one stage removed from the local peasant communities in which most had been born. In contrast to the localized secret society lodge, they were rootless, roving, permanently
outside of society. Such bandits were linked to the more quiescent
secret societies sometimes by personal ties or by nominal commitment to shared quasi-religious rituals, but most importantly by the
common political and economic grievances of their predominantly
lower class members against officials and gentry. The tsei brotherhoods were thus potentially the cadres of an expanded rebel movement
which could challenge the imperial state not just on the local level,
but even for the control of a province or a greater geographical region. The Nien rebellion in north China was fed precisely by social

circumstances of this kind, as were the multiple secret society insurrections in south China before and after the movement of the Taipings
from Kwangsi to Nanking.   And both Shih Tai-k'ai, after he was ex-
pelled from the Taiping captial, and Li Hsiu-ch'eng in east China in
the early 1860s assumed some of the characteristics of bandits as
the influence of the original Taiping ideology upon them was weakened.

As a further confirmation of the ambiguous definition of social
collectivities in rural China below the formal structure of bureaucratic
government which I have noted several times in the foregoing discussion, bandit gangs were sometimes a source from which officials or
local elite enlisted loyal mercenaries (yung) to suppress the mounting
disorder which they faced.   The phenomena of "pacification" and "turn-
coats" were thus not only a function of an ideological indeterminacy
which I have already set forth, but also of changing balances of power
and clashing personal ambitions in a local society which the state did
not directly control.

A HIERARCHY OF DISSIDENCE

Aggravated social strain reflected with various degrees of clarity by a discordant ideology onto a potentially rebellious collectivity: this is the etiology of rebellion whose abstract boxes I have attempted to fill with specimens from late-Ch'ing China. Social dissidence in the nineteenth century characteristically originated in Chinese society below the thin layer of direct bureaucratic government which penetrated little beyond the level of the hsien. The countryside, only indirectly controlled by the imperial state, had social contours of its own, long-lived or thrown up in response to the deterioration of local order which began symbolically with the White Lotus rebellion. Although not recorded in the statutes of the realm, the Ta-Ch'ing hui-tien, lineages, militia, villages, sects, and secret societies--all of them were foci of social organization as "legitimate" as the bureaucratic divisions which the empire imposed upon the "natural" local society. Sometimes indistinctly outlined, capable of being transformed into their apparent opposites, these collectivities to some degree were linked to the imperial state, by shared values or by institutionalized controls, but they were not mere arms of a totalitarian regime. In troubled times, when personal, family, class, or local interests seemed to demand it, they could become the foci of resistance and even of rebellion against the imperial system, and sometimes also challenge--as yet mildly, in the nineteenth century--the structure of the local society in which they were embedded.

Festering and fermenting in the rural villages, only occasionally did rebellion become entrenched and widespread enough to challenge the imperial state even at the local level. Control, compromise, or bloody repression were more often effective than not in containing the political and social tensions of the countryside. Even at the pinnacle of the Taiping movement, the greatest rebellion in geographical scope and intensity of combat before the twentieth century, there were substantial areas of the contested Yangtze valley provinces which were hardly affected at all. All the oppressed and exploited did not rise up en masse under the Taiping banner to overthrow the imperial state and gentry society. The soldiers of Tseng Kuo-fan's Hunan Army were mostly peasants too, not unlike the rank and file of the rebel armies whom they defeated. The reasons for the ability of the dynasty to withstand even these unprecedented adversaries I shall analyze

73

below. In the present context, I wish to suggest that the Taipings
stood highest in a hierarchy of dissident movements which arose out
of the social and economic strains and the political exhaustion of
nineteenth-century China. And only the Taipings came near to success; the others, as we move down the hierarchy, were progressively
more easily overwhelmed by the weight of the traditional state and
society.

It is not difficult, from the empirical evidence of lesser or
greater threat to the dynasty, to describe a hierarchy of socially
dissident movements. Less obvious is what distinguished one level
of action and organization from another, or what in addition was
needed to transform one level of rebellion into another of higher
intensity. Because I have analyzed rebellion as a possible consequence of social strain, it must seem to follow that an increment
of strain produces an increment of rebelliousness. There is probably some such correlation, if we knew how to measure it, but I
am reluctant to conclude that the essential ingredient was "social
strain" in general, rather than specific kinds of strain. Economic
distress might appear a likely candidate, were it not for the widespread observation that extreme famine normally inhibits rather than
stimulates opposition movements. Radical impoverishment keeps a
population too busy scratching for food, clothing, and shelter--in
order merely to survive--for it to organize rebellion. What to look
for, I suggest, is an unusual and growing degree of political exhaustion: an inability of the polity to utilize what to the observer appears
as its substantial resources to control disorder. Greater "corruption"
as I explained that term earlier, seemed to induce greater dissidence
A second variable shaping our hierarchy is the intensity of the ideological confrontation with the traditional social order: how thorough
were the criticisms, with what precision were alternatives and programs for their realization presented? Possibly radical ideology was
correlated with the exhaustion of the polity under attack; the decay of
the ideological "integuement" from within made it increasingly susceptible to external assault.

It is probable that a third variable, the extent to which a rebel
lious movement was separated from the on-going normal activities of
the local community, also was related to the degree to which the
social order had begun to exhaust its political resources. The ability
of a dissident movement to detach itself physically from the legal society which its legitimate adversary controlled, to avoid both immedia

repression and the inducements to compromise which were the accompaniments of continuing to function in that society, could give it the time and space to discover and experiment with alternative forms of social organization. A weakening polity made such an exodus a possibility. In the longer run, the traditional society could be confronted head on not just by organized violence, but also by the promise of a new society which in embryo was already in being. Reculer pour mieux sauter. Encircling the cities from the countryside. The echoes of this theme were to carry over into the twentieth century, as we shall see, and, greatly amplified, it would marshall the forces of the Chinese Communist Party against the Japanese invader, against the Kuomintang, against the imperialist world. For the Taipings and others its measures brought more ambiguous results.

At the base of the hierarchy of dissidence stand ad hoc acts of individuals or small group protest which normally had no lasting social effects. Directed against oppressive landlords or corrupt local officials, these demonstrations or riots had next to no organization or ideology and sought only the righting of individual wrongs. The participants were local people, well-known to each other in many day-to-day contexts, and their targets were the elite of their own communities. Refusal to pay oppressive rents or taxes, and hunger riots were common forms in which this level of dissidence expressed itself. In the following example, from Yü-yao, Chekiang, in 1858, antigentry protest burgeoned into an antiofficial riot:

> Yü-yao is situated on the seacoast, where the inhabitants are ferocious, and wealthy families are accustomed to oppressing the common people. Last year, some inhabitants went to the hsien [yamen] to report a famine; they petitioned that rent be reduced. The magistrate, Ts'ui Chia-yin, listened to them. [With his authorization] an association was promptly formed and a bureau established; special dry-measures were made to be used in rent collection. Three of the "big families," Shao, Hung, and Hsieh, refused to comply [with the new arrangements]. Violent fights broke out immediately.

> It happened that at this juncture a new magistrate arrived [at Yü-yao to replace Ts'ui Chia-yin]. The Shao family, in conjunction with others, forced the new magistrate to recruit local militiamen and to order them to arrest the

tenants; they increased the rent further, inscribed the
new rates on stone tablets, set up special bureaus
[to collect the rent], and demanded prompt payment
[from the tenants]. The rural inhabitants were infu-
riated. Hsüan Hsi-wen and Huang Ch'un-sheng, both
"bandits," together with some others, incited the tenants
to make trouble. After having surrounded and burned
down the homes of some of the wealthy people, the mob
attacked the hsien city in the same evening and set free
[all the tenants] that were previously imprisoned [by the
new magistrate] (Li Tzu-ming, Yüeh-man-t'ang jih-chi pu
[Supplement to his diary], Shanghai, 1936, ssu-chi, p. 6a,
trans. in Kung-chuan Hsiao, Rural China: Imperial Control
in the Nineteenth Century, Seattle: University of Washington Press, 1960, p. 429, additions in original).

In most such cases the ringleaders would be apprehended and execute
in the market place. The above uprising was quelled with much bloo
shed.

Interlineage and communal feuds (the two might overlap, as in
the case of many Hakka-Punti clashes) were also usually localized an
without explicit political ideologies on either side. I place them next
in the hierarchy of dissidence because they sometimes were conducte
on a considerable scale, and because they could very well escalate
into genuine rebellion if one of the parties came to identify itself wit
a heretical religious ideology while the other called upon official sup-
port--as we know happened in Kwangsi in the early stages of what
became the Taiping rebellion. The normal content of these feuds
(hsieh-tou, "weapons fights," they were commonly called) might be
the Chinese equivalent of south European "blood vengeance," ethnic
conflict, or very commonly struggles between villages (and lineages,
when they coincided) for the control of water rights. These last
contained at least an implicit class conflict, in that the larger and
richer lineages often preyed on the poorer and smaller. Consider
the following example, from Kwangtung:

On a plain that I have often traversed, north of Swatow,
there was a few years ago, a little village inhabited by
a small and weak clan [i.e., lineage], surnamed Stone
[Shih]. There were twelve neighboring villages, chiefly
of the Plum [Mei] clan, and these all combined against

the Stones, whom they far outnumbered. The Stones
planted and watered their crops, and the Plums reaped
the harvest. There were perpetual raids on the property of the Stones, and they, having no redress for
their wrongs were in danger of utter extinction (Adele
Marion Fielde, A Corner of Cathay: Studies From Life
Among the Chinese, New York, 1894, p. 128, quoted by
Hsiao, Rural China, p. 367, additions in original).

The response of the victims could be an alliance of poorer villages,
which might enlarge the violence and bring the local magistrate onto
the scene. Official repression in turn could nudge some of the original actors into rebellion.

Although the sharing of rituals and passwords created an underworld network of communications which could range over many provinces,
the secret society lodge per se was locally oriented and often more involved in rackets than rebellion. If, by being secret, the lodge was
not precisely "in" local society, with respect to membership and activities it was certainly "of" it. Similarly the heretical sect typically
was closely associated with the folk cult of a specific locale. Both
had the potential of being incorporated into larger nonlocalized movements, but the religious and secular "underworld" in its more quiescent phases places next in the hierarchy principally because of its
antiestablishment ideology. Often diluted or murky, to be sure,
vague millenarian Buddhism-Taoism-folk religion and anti-Manchu
Ming restorationism were criticisms at least of political practice if
not of the underlying society. As these organizations were also potentially mobilizable by what they could perceive as a threat to the
traditional society as a whole--which accounts for the secret society
role in the anti-Christian incidents which punctuated the last half of
the nineteenth century--their ideological ambiguity should simultaneously be noted.

At the next step up the hierarchy are located those bandit gangs
(tsei) described earlier. Ideologically vague, some at least shared
their outlook with the secret societies and sects. But, unlike the
"normal" underworld, the bandit gangs by necessity or by choice were
detached from a particular local community. Most were no more than
criminals, preying on the lao-pai-hsing as much as on the elite.
Others--groups of substantial scale and with a "professional" corps of
leaders, their separation symbolized (and enforced: beware to be cap-

tured sans the usual shaved forehead) by long hair or a lotus tattooed on their faces--saw a political future for themselves. Such was the origin of Li Tzu-ch'eng who overthrew the Ming, and probably also of Sung Ching-shih whose Shantung bandit forces played off the Ch'ing and the Nien against each other in the 1860s while augmenting their own power by raiding the countryside. At the peak of his influence in 1863, Sung led as many as 30,000 men and briefly challenged the dynasty for the control of a substantial part of Shantung.

The next two steps are, first, rebellion, and then, at the apex of the hierarchy, revolution. Somewhere between rebellion and revolution we find the Taipings; all the rest were merely rebels. If we consider both the extent of the territory outside of the imperial writ which they attempted to control and within which some tiny sprouts of a new society blossomed very briefly; and also the intensity of their ideological attack on Ch'ing state and society, the Taipings were as revolutionary a movement as China saw before the twentieth century. Those dissident movements that were more strictly rebellions were similar to the Taipings in kind but not in degree in the matter of their divorce from the routine life patterns of rural China. Some faintly shared even the millenarianism of the God-worshippers. Only the latter, however, began to incorporate into its ideology not only a rejection of the present evil world and a chiliastic belief (in the second coming of Christ's younger brother, if not of Jesus himself), but also the rudiments of a social program, of a system of political organization, of a practical method for achieving power. But only the rudiments. And that is why even the Taiping Kingdom does not occupy the very top of the hierarchy of social dissidence: in ascending order--ad hoc local riots; lineage and communal feuds with a potentiality for escalation; the religious and political underworld contingently linked to broader ambitions; politicalized bandits; rebellion which can suck into its whirlpool lesser forms of dissidence; and unqualified political and social revolution.

THE SUPPRESSION AND CONSEQUENCES OF REBELLION

Why Rebellion Failed

The nineteenth-century rebellions failed to overthrow the Ch'ing dynasty primarily because they were ideologically and organizationally unable to destroy the remarkable equilibrium between the two interpenetrating levels of the Chinese political system. At the center of this equilibrium stood what we have agreed to call the Confucian gentry. Their ideology justified the Confucian-Legalist imperial state (Level I of the polity), and sanctioned the orthodox tests and examining institutions by means of which the more academically qualified among them were selected to staff the offices of the state bureaucracy. Simultaneously this ideology legitimized the gentry--those not in office --as the dominant social, economic, and political elite in Chinese local society, beneath the broad but shallow overlay of the imperial state whose writ rarely penetrated below the level of the 1,500 chou and hsien magistrates appointed by the emperor (Level II of the polity). Confucian raison d'état and Confucian "general will," as I have termed them, produced an equilibrium in tension which normally could absorb severe shocks and even accommodate some institutional change without impairing the basic integration and stability of the political and social systems.

Each depended on the other: the nonofficial gentry needed the imperial state, its endorsement of Confucian orthodoxy, its examination system and bureaucratic structures which provided them with degrees, titles, and privileges upon which much of their local social status was based; the state needed the gentry as the source of orthodoxly indoctrinated officials, and for their performance of informal but critical political functions in their local communities (arbitration of disputes, the organization of charity, upkeep of temples and lineage halls, teaching, local self-defense, and sometimes even tax collection). If for no other reason than because premodern technology, especially in the means of communication, ruled it out of the question, a centralized authoritarian state governing from a single center and reaching into the farthest corner of society with detailed prescriptive regulations was an impossibility. China's rural society, its hundreds of millions of peasants in a hundred thousand villages, were "ruled" not by a few tens of thousands of imperial bureaucrats, but by a local "ruling class" consisting of a million gentry members and their families.

Relatively isolated instances of insurrection at the lower end of the hierarchy of social dissidence, though they might attack both officials and gentry as in the examples I have given, were normally quickly suppressed. When, in the first half of the nineteenth century there was a general breakdown of social order, the multiplication of such incidents and the inability of the polity to respond adequately to them produced heightened social tension, rebellion of a more threatening mien, and even quasi-revolution in the case of the Taiping Heavenly Kingdom.

With the exception of the Taipings, the rebellions of the nineteenth-century only superficially attacked either the imperial state or gentry-dominated local society. Vague millenarianism and Ming restorationism, as in the case of the White Lotus uprisings; the resentment of the Miao and Muslim national and religious-ethnic minorities against Han-Manchu chauvinism; antidynastic political bandits like the Nien--these gave rise to insurrections involving large numbers of peasants and other lower class persons which, however troubling to the government, did not make a radical ideological attack on the Confucian cultural integuement which, as it were, rationalized the political and social status quo. They might prove difficult to pacify --nine years for the White Lotus, eighteen years each for the Miao and Nien, twenty-four years for the Muslim rebellions--but part of the reason that these rebellions were so long sustained is that they were "traditional," familiar types of opposition with whose inherent limitations both officials and gentry were familiar. There was, in other words, perhaps a less than total urgency to divert the resource required for their defeat, a wavering between possible political conciliation and military suppression.

In the cases of the contemporaneous Miao, Muslims, and Nien, confrontation with the Taiping uprising also obviously took precedence for the imperial state, and thus these smaller threats survived longer than they would have in the absence of Hung Hsiu-ch'üan's Heavenly Kingdom. And, as a third factor accounting for their longevity, I have noted the organizational and technical "exhaustion" of the Banner and Green Standard regular army in the face of endemic and increasing local disorder. Without these special circumstances, there is nothing to suggest that any except the Taiping rebellion had the potential to survive very long.

I have already implied that it is easy to have doubts about treating the White Lotus and Nien uprisings as unified movements;

and difficult to accept the inflated official reports about their numbers. The same hesitations are probably in order with respect to the Miao uprising. In any case, the leadership of all three was of a quasi-bandit character, without the capacity to give ideological cohesion or a stable political organization to their fragmented adherents. (The Muslim uprisings, which sometimes expressed Islamic religious ambitions, were in practice directed against specific political and economic abuses, and not fundamentally against either the imperial state or the organization of society.) Nor was the popular support which these rebellions clearly sometimes obtained unqualified or deeply rooted; without long-range political goals and precise political organization, that kind of support was unobtainable. And finally, however adept at guerrilla warfare he might be, no rebel could overthrow the empire by such tactics alone. To sum up: traditional peasant rebellion can be put down by military means (and some palliatives) so long as the ancien regime, though it may be inefficient and corrupt, has retained a belief in its values and ideology and can sustain even creakily functioning police and military institutions.

The Taiping movement was a quantum leap ahead of its contemporaries. Not a modern social revolution, but potentially much more than vague millenarianism, secret society restorationism, or anti-dynastic banditry. For the first time since the absorption and neutralization of Buddhism in medieval China, a challenge was being raised to the ideology which sustained both Level I and Level II of the polity. It was a two-pronged challenge. Taiping Christianity cum utopianism directly attacked the equilibrium between Confucian raison d'état (the universal and specific interests of the centralized empire, its monarch, and his chief officials) and Confucian "general will" (the particular and diffuse interests of the rural gentry) which I believe was the key to the long-lived existence of the imperial state. It also assailed the Confucian ideological justification for the institutions in both halves of the equilibrium, and thus opened the institutions themselves to attack.

The first prong, the idea of a theocratic state ruled by a monarch whose legitimacy was derived from a transcendental God and who was not--as a Manchu emperor, or a Ming or Sung Han Chinese emperor before him, was--himself dependent upon the ideology of the Confucian gentry, threatened to extend the power of the state directly into local society. It raised the ideological possibility of--I have suggested the analogy of Petrine Russia--an étatist effort to dominate society (all-out bureaucratic "Legalism" to use an old Chinese term) which could circumvent or modify or eliminate the special position of the Confucian gentry as the local ruling class. The second prong, by bringing forth the utopian visions of a heterodox stream of Confucian thought, questioned whether either the institutions of the bureaucratic state or those of local society were in fact adequate representations of the basic values of Chinese civilization. It offered egalitarian alternatives in such critical matters as landholding and even daily consumption (the "common treasuries") which would remove the traditional elite entirely from the scene and substitute a single religious-political-military hierarchy of officials.

A problem arises at this point. Little of the Taiping utopian ideology was ever translated into distinctive institutions, and the major documents setting out these ideas and outlining implementation were mainly published in 1854 and earlier. Are we to conclude that the later years of the Heavenly Kingdom saw the decline of an early egalitarian spirit, or alternatively that the utopian egalitarian current in the Taiping movement was distinctly a secondary one, that Hung was essentially a demented religious sectarian? I am inclined to accept the latter characterization. But even Hung's religious message by itself presented a challenge to state and society of unprecedented seriousness. And while we may discount the practical relevance of the <u>Land System of the Heavenly Dynasty</u>, the more rational though still naive <u>New Work for Aid in Government</u> authored by Hung Jen-kan called for a "modernization" of Chinese society which would be as fatal to the Confucian elite as the equal land distribution of the <u>Land System</u>.

Tseng Kuo-fan, the central figure in the suppression of the mid-nineteenth century rebellions, was acutely aware that the Taipings threatened not just the dynasty, as traditional rebels had done, but the preservation of "civilization" (<u>ming-chiao</u>). He launched his campaign against the rebels by issuing a "Proclamation Against the Bandits of Kwangtung and Kwangsi" in February 1854 whose virulent intensity matches contemporary Taiping attacks on the Ch'ing; an excerpt follows:

> Since the time of T'ang, Yü, and the Three Dynasties,
> the sage men of each age have sustained our culture and
> civilization (<u>ming-chiao</u>) and emphasized the proper order-
> ing of human relationships. Thus, the positions of ruler
> and officials, father and children, high and low, honored
> and humble, were as established in their respective places

as a hat and shoes which can never be interchanged. Now
the Kwangtung and Kwangsi bandits have appropriated some
of the cultural refuse of the foreign barbarians and adhere
to the religion of God. From their false king and false
ministers down to the rank and file soldiers and lowest ser-
vants, they address one another as brothers, and allege that
only Heaven can be called father. Moreover, all the fathers
among the people are brothers, and all the mothers sisters.

The peasants cannot cultivate their own fields and pay taxes,
because it is held that all the land belongs to the Heavenly
King. The merchants cannot pursue their own businesses
and make profits, because it is held that all commodities
are the property of the Heavenly King. The scholars cannot read the Confucian classics, but only the New Testament.
In brief, the moral system, human ethical relationships, cultural inheritance, and institutions of the past several thousand
years are swept away in one stroke. This is not simply a
calamity for our great Ch'ing dynasty, but the most extraordinary upheaval since the establishment of Chinese culture
and civilization in ancient times. This is what Confucius
and Mencius are bitterly crying about in the nether world.
How can any who read books and know the written charac-
ters sit with their hands in their sleeves without doing something about it? (Trans. from text in Chien Yu-wen, T'ai-
p'ing t'ien-kuo ch'üan-shih [Complete history of the Taiping
rebellion], Hong Kong, 1962, vol. 2, pp. 1083-85.)

Tseng's message was clear: if the imperial state were destroyed by
the rebels, the ideological and political basis of the Confucian gentry
would also be undermined; if Confucianism were lost, gentry and bureaucracy, emperor and dynasty--all would be lost. If, as some
writers have suggested, there still remained deep but muted antagonisms between Chinese and Manchus, they were subordinated to this
greater common threat.

The dynasty was saved, and Confucian culture and gentry-dominated local society with it, when Tseng and other gentry leaders
rallied to its cause. It must not be concluded that the dynasty and
imperial state automatically welcomed the enhanced role of the gentry,
and the accretion of political, economic, and military power to local
interests that necessarily accompanied their assumption of the major
responsibility for pacifying the Taiping, Nien, Miao, and Muslim re-

bellions. On the contrary, such devolution was seen by the court and the Peking bureaucracy as temporary, necessary in their desperation but unfortunate. Over the particulars of the facilities which Tseng and other gentry leaders sought to appropriate for their own use there were fierce political struggles, with now the state and now local power centers in the ascendancy. So long, however, as the imperial state by its own traditional means was unable to quell the insurgents, it could not dispense with Tseng, Li Hung-chang, and Tso Tung-t'ang and others who came to command the only effective prodynastic military forces in China. As we have seen, the Banners and Green Standard battalions of the Ch'ing regular army, both because of deficiencies in their basic organization and deployment and as a consequence of corruption and demoralization, failed to contain the proliferating rebellions. The dynasty, moreover, in the last half of the 1850s was preoccupied with a serious external challenge from the treaty powers which ended with the latter employing military force to coerce additional commercial and political privileges from Peking. And finally, pacification of the major rebellions required a rehabilitation of local society and restoration of "law and order" which had proved beyond the competence of the imperial state but might be accomplished by the gentry themselves.

However much greater an ideological threat than any other of the mid-century rebellions the Taiping movement was, and notwithstanding its control of substantial territories which furnished the men and supplies for a formidable military organization, the Heavenly Kingdom was unable to mobilize the political means to unseat the gentry who dominated rural society. This radical political weakness, and the more immediate factors I have already noted, were fatal to the rebellion. Though Level I of the Ch'ing polity showed manifest signs of "exhaustion," Level II under the leadership of Tseng Kuo-fan evidenced a vigor and resilience sufficient to neutralize and then demolish the Taiping challenge.

I am tempted to summarize the Taiping political failure as the incapacity to mobilize, indoctrinate, and deploy systematically a sufficiently large corps of political cadres to bring the countryside under the direct control of the insurgent leadership. From this lacun there followed a number of untoward consequences. First, their Confucian gentry rivals remained in control of much of rural society even in those areas which were dominated by Taiping military garrisons. Some of the local elite perforce cooperated with the rebels by serving as they had in the past, as agents for the collection and remission of taxes; others played off the Taipings against the imperial forces for their own benefit; most frequently, the local gentry became the foci for intense resistance against the Taipings which prevented the rebel writ from extending very far outside the walls of the cities they had captured.

Their inability to penetrate and control rural society meant, secondly, that the Taipings were unable to recruit or conscript adequate manpower for their armies. The numerical strength of the Taiping forces was often exaggerated in the reports of the officials who unsuccessfully undertook to defeat them. There were probably no more than 50,000 full-time combattants in the great horde which descended on Nanking in 1853; this may have been one reason why no garrisons could be left in the cities taken on the route of march, why the expedition sent against Peking was so small, why the Taipings did not proceed against Shanghai in 1853, and why they did not directly aid the contemporary Nien, Muslim, and Miao insurrections. After 1860, the Taiping armies appear to have been considerably larger, but they no longer had the intensity of ideological commitment which had characterized the original Kwangsi-Kwangtung recruits. Banditti, local bullies, victims of the civil war, lumpen elements of many varieties, had been absorbed for example by the forces of Shih Ta-k'ai and Li Hsiu-ch'eng.

This last development is related to a third consequence of the Taiping political failure: a general decline in the religious fervor which had provided the basis for the political integration of the rebellion. Restricted in its unadulterated strength to a small core of true-believers, the original God-worshippers, and unable to attract from local society in newly conquered areas a continuous stream of equally committed adherents who could provide new vigor, ideas, and leadership, Taiping Christianity turned in on itself and became increasingly sterile. Most of the rebel publications after 1854 were merely reissues, sometimes with small revisions, of the flood of doctrinal works which appeared in the first years of the rebellion. It is here that we have at least a partial explanation for the otherwise troublesome fact that--apart from faint echoes, for example, in the early career of Sun Yat-sen whose veracity one should accept only with caution-- the great Taiping floodtide which had swept up so many millions in its turbulence receded and left no ideological trace after the recapture of Nanking in 1864. I am not aware of any intellectual disciples of Hung Hsiu-chüan preaching his gospel in the remaining decades of the Manchu dynasty. That contorted message in its full doctrinal and emotional meaning had never been diffused beyond the God-worshippers from Kwangsi and Kwnagtung who were massacred to the last man by Tseng Kuo-ch'üan's victorious soldiers.

The decay of the source of Taiping political integration, and the inability to institutionalize a working alternative government appointed from the rebel political center in the territories that they dominated militarily led, fourthly, to the phenomenon of quasi-banditry which I have already noted. After 1856, the ties of Shih Ta-k'ai's roving forces to the original Taiping movement were increasingly only historical; although Li Hsiu-ch'eng in east China in the early 1860s was never so completely cut off from Nanking, he too operated increasingl as a semi-independent warlord. Finally, not having penetrated and reorganized rural society in the utopian image of their early tracts, the Taipings after the conquest of Nanking in 1853 had no stronger appeal with which to garner popular support than ·did Tseng Kuo-fan. The latter, in fact, by drawing upon the traditional Confucian theme of peasant welfare as the foundation of society, could in the short-run retrieve the allegience of the rural population which the economic and political strains of the early nineteenth century had alienated.

But why were the Taipings unsuccessful in supplanting the Confucian local gentry with Taiping local cadres? Of especial importance I believe, were the deficiencies of the sources, Chinese and foreign, from which they somewhat incoherently constructed their ideology. Neither Christianity nor the ta-t'ung tradition provided any guidance for the modern political mobilization with which we have become familiar. Even if Hung's primitive Christian thought had not repelled the Confucian gentry--see Tseng Kuo-fan's 1854 proclamation quoted above--the Taiping movement still lacked any practical conception of how to win political power that genuinely differed from that which the Chinese tradition, from which its leaders could never fully escape, provided. In a deep and meaningful way, the Taiping rebellion did confront Confucian China with a radical alternative, but the threat remained abstract--ideological--because the rebels had no effective doctrine about how to achieve the transfer of power. Mao Tse-tung, in this case, was correct in arguing that without "the leadership . . . of an advanced political party" Chinese peasant rebellions invariably failed. The Taipings were not a "modern" political movement; their government in Nanking aped the externals of that in Peking, and adde(the archaism of competing personal appanages of the several kings which the bureaucratic imperial state of the Ch'ing period did not tolerate in its capital.

The harnessing of the social strains which produced radical but premodern rebellion to the cause of modern social revolution was eventually accomplished in twentieth-century China. For this result, the preconditions were not only the growth of the technological means ("communications" in the broadest sense) to bring a new message to the Chinese people which would weld them into a nation, and the trial and error perfection of a political strategy for their mobilization, but also a fundamental shift in the relationships between the state and society, Level I and Level II of the polity as I have called them. This the nineteenth-century rebellions failed to achieve. Paradoxically, while the short-range issue of the rallying the Confucian gentry to the defense of the Ch'ing dynasty was a refurbishment of that equilibrium which had produced the long-lived Chinese political system, in the longer run forces were set in motion which were to be disequilibrating. Together with the consequences of the augmented foreign impact on China after 1860, these were sufficient to bring the dynasty to an end and to open up the question of what the shape of the underlying Chinese society should be. The beginnings of this portentous change can be traced to the organization of the Hunan Army by Tseng Kuo-fan.

Tseng Kuo-fan and the Hunan Army

Tseng Kuo-fan (1811-1872) has been much reviled in recent Chinese Communist historiography as a "traitor and executioner," who betrayed the interests of the Chinese people by his support of the Manchu dynasty and brutally crushed the popular rebellions of the mid-nineteenth century. That Tseng was deeply influenced by the authoritarian strain in Sung Neo-Confucianism which emphasized the importance of social hierarchy is evident enough from the proclamation of 1854 from which I quoted earlier. His brutality in dealing with the banditti of Hunan and his policy of exterminating the Taipings and other rebels are also a matter of record. The accusation that Tseng deliberately chose to ignore the anti-Manchu nationalism of the Taipings which occurs also in Non-Marxist Chinese critiques, does however beg the question. It is, I believe, an anachronistic reading back into the 1850s of what we might call the Kuomintang version of China's modern history, i.e., one which sees the major issue of the late-

Ch'ing as the struggle of Han Chinese nationalism against an alien Manchu dynasty. While such an interpretation may help to establish the legitimacy of the Kuomintang claim to continuous leadership of modern Chinese nationalism, it does violence to the facts of Manchu acculturation to suggest that the matter of an alien dynasty was a salient question among either Chinese intellectuals or peasants in the middle of the nineteenth century. The Taipings of course were anti-Manchu, but for this appeal to be politically meaningful the dynasty first had to lose its legitimacy on other grounds, in particular by its inability to withstand the onrush of foreign imperialism. Although long in gestation, this last became a critical issue only at the end of the century.

Tseng was born in Hsiang-hsiang, Hunan, the eldest son of a qu: poor gentry family whose scholarly credentials did not extend back beyond his grandfather's generation. His father, a village teacher, beca a sheng-yuan only in 1832--after sixteen previous failures in the exam inations. Kuo-fan won the same degree a year later, became a chü-je in 1834, and in 1838, at age twenty-eight, passed the chin-shih examination and became a member of the Han-lin Academy. His subsequer meteoric rise in the Peking bureaucracy--in 1849 he became junior vice-president of the Board of Rites--was a product of both his scholarly brilliance and the backing of the influential Manchu scholar of Sung Neo-Confucianism, Mu-chang-a (1782-1856). With many important friends in the capital and strong local ties, it is understandable that Tseng (who in 1853 had returned home to observe the customary mourning period for his recently deceased mother) should have been among those retired officials and locally important gentry ordered by the court to organize militia in support of the provincial defense forces who had been unable to stem the Taiping advance from Hunan into Hupei.

There was a hidden agenda behind this imperial order. In fact, the process of local militarization was well underway by 1853; in Huna for example, Chiang Chung-yuan (1812-1854) had organized a militia in Hsin-ning as early as 1847 to cope with local disorders. Chiang reac tivated his force in 1851 when the Taiping rebellion broke out. Lo Ts nan (1808-1856), like Tseng from Hsiang-hsiang district, had raised a militia in 1852 to defend Changsha against the advancing rebel armies. These examples were only the most prominent among many similar instances of gentry-organized t'uan-lien and yung in these turbulent years, a phenomenon discussed earlier in this essay. What the court sought was not only to bolster the flaccid regular army, but also to gain control of the nonofficial armed units under gentry leadership which had burgeoned in the fact of growing local disorder. What Tseng Kuo-fan eventually fashioned went a long distance beyond the court's intention to regularize and coopt the numerous localized t'uan-lien. His strategic aims were not to be limited only to his home district or even to his province. The Hunan Army (Hsiang-chün) and its offshoot, Li Hung-chang's Huai Army (Huai-chün), became in fact if not de jure the only effective "regular" military forces facing the mid-century rebellions. And, unlike the Banners and Green Standard battalions, these new armies were only nominally subject to the bureaucratic control of the Peking authorities. The loyalty of Tseng and Li and their collaborators to the Ch'ing dynasty was never in question, but a shift in the balance of power, in the equilibrium between the imperial state and gentry dominated local society, was initiated.

The original nuclei of Tseng's army were the militia forces of Lo Tse-nan and Chiang Chung-yuan. These were yung-level (i.e., not localized village self-defense units) battalions whose commanders, scholarly soldiers from Hunan, were well-known to Tseng and personally loyal to him. The officers and rank and file had been recruited through a pyramid of personal loyalties extending down to the village t'uan-lien which provided the basic manpower pool. Tseng enlarged his force by bringing into the coalition additonal yung-type battalions, each again under leaders with whom he had significant personal ties (kinship, common locality, friendship, and the like). Among the important political and military figures of late-Ch'ing China who first rose to prominence in Tseng Kuo-fan's military camp were such men as Tso Tung-t'ang (1812-1885), Tseng Kuo-ch'üan (1824-1890), P'eng Yü-lin (1816-1890), and Liu K'un-i (1830-1902), all of Hunan; and Li Hung-chang (1823-1901) of Anhwei. Of the 182 highest officers of the Hunan Army who have left biographical records, 125 (69 per cent) were from the province of Hunan; 65 (36 per cent) held examination degrees; fourteen later held the post of governor-general, thirteen became governors, and 131 held other lower official positions. At its peak size the Hunan Army numbered about 120,000 men. Tseng and his officers made a determined effort to nurture a sense of loyalty and commitment to their units among the rank and file, to indoctrinate them with Confucian virtues, and to pay their troops regularly and on a higher scale than the Green Standard army.

The Hunan Army's expansion after 1853 was relatively slow, not only because of Tseng Kuo-fan's deliberate leadership and careful screening of new recruits, but also because of substantial difficulties in raising funds and obtaining equipment and supplies. In theory the new force consisted of "official braves" who were to be paid and main tained by the imperial government along with its regular troops. In practice, the higher provincial officials reluctantly cooperated in maki these resources available; the court, as it gradually learned of the re scope of Tseng's actions, was not yet ready to underwrite so great a devolution of military power out of its hands. Moreover, some leade of local t'uan-lien resisted the incorporation of their men into Tseng's army and the accompanying diversion of revenue from the local to higher levels.

To finance the growing Hunan Army in its early years, as well as a naval force planned to wrest control of the Yangtze waterway from the Taipings, Tseng and his gentry allies had to rely on their own political and personal connections to garner local land tax receipts, received some "contributions" in exchange for the granting of official rank, illegally diverted funds intended for the regular troops, and began to collect an ad valorem tax on goods in transit (likin). The problem of adequately financing the Hunan Army was not solved until May 1860 when Tseng at last received a substantive official appointment which gave him legal access to the regular taxes. On becoming governor-general of Liang-Chiang (the provinces of Kiangsu, Kiangsi, and Anhwei) and imperial commissioner for the suppression of the Taipings, the rich revenues of these provinces (including the growing customs receipts of Shanghai) and likin came under his control; thereafter they were the principal support of both the Hunan and the Huai Armies. Tseng received this appointment, however, only after repeated Taiping victories had brought the court and the Peking bureaucracy to the edge of desperation.

Before 1860 the Hunan Army had a mixed record of victories and defeats in battles fought in Hunan, Hupei, and Kiangsi provinces. With the fall of Anking in September 1861, the tide definitely turned in the war area west of Nanking where Tseng Kuo-fan had taken direct charge. At the same time Li Hung-chang (who in 1853 had been sent home from his post in the Han-lin Academy to organize local militia in Anhwei, which he did until joining Tseng's army in 1858) emerged as the commander of a new military organization modelled on the Hunan Army. The Huai Army was recruited largely in Anhwei province by incorporating existing yung battalions such as that led by Liu Ming-ch'uan (1836-1896). Tseng had entrusted Li with its organization in part in response to pressure from the gentry of Kiangsu for a force adequate to recover the east China cities from Li Hsiu-ch'eng; the army was then to move against Nanking from the east. On Tseng's recommendation Li became governor of Kiangsu, which insured formal access to the revenues required to support the Huai Army. Tseng apparently had an additional motive in encouraging the establishment of this organizationally separate force by his lieutenant. In spite of the formal recognition which the failure of its regular army had forced Peking to give him, Tseng was aware that his growing power had created great jealousies and even fear. He hoped that he might be able to maintain his influence in the future if it were exercised more indirectly--through the informal control of an army headed by a second person--than his current command of the Hunan Army.

After the defeat of the Taipings in 1864, the court in fact made several attempts to reduce Tseng's influence and that of Li, in effect to recover the power which had devolved into the hands of the gentry leaders of provincial and regional armies. Although he kept his position as governor-general, Tseng Kuo-fan found it expedient to demobilize most of his Hunan Army before the end of 1864. Several thousand troops were also discharged from the Huai Army. Had it not been for the death of Seng-ko-lin-ch'in and the decimation of his army in 1865, which made Peking dependent upon Tseng Kuo-fan and Li Hung-chang to defeat the Nien rebels, a further reduction of their military and political power might have been anticipated. When Tseng was sent to command the anti-Nien armies in Honan, it was agreed that Li Hung-chang would substitute for him as acting Liang-Chiang governor-general. The Peking authorities, however, tried to back out of this agreement, and without the aggravated Nien threat which required the intercession of the Huai Army might have been able to remove Li and reassert central control over the key Kiangnan area and its revenues. The protracted conflict with the Nien--even the Huai Army could not bring an immediate victory--provided a pretext for an effort to replace Li Hung-chang with a Manchu general which was also abortive.

These developments are evidence that important changes had occurred in the relations between central and provincial authority which were not accepted with equanimity by Peking. But enhanced provincial prerogatives vis-à-vis the capital is not by itself the equivalent of a shift to greater local gentry power as against the imperial state. By assuming high provincial office, gentry leaders like Tseng, Li, and Tso in effect refashioned the old links which tied the gentry to the formal governmental structure. As in the past, these "official gentry" or "bureaucractic gentry" played overlapping roles: they were simultaneously officials appointed by and loyal to the central government, and the "representatives" in that government of the much more numerous "nonofficial gentry" who were the political and social elite of rural China. In addition to an alteration on the central-provincial balance, what had also begun to change were the respective weights of central and local influence on the men in high provincial office. Although some, Li Hung-chang for example, were later to identify themselves more with the interests of the imperial state (Confucian raison d'état) than with those of the local rural gentry (Confucian "general will"), a further consequence of the rebellions and the manner in which Tseng and Li in the Yangtze provinces, and Tso Tsung-t'ang in the northwest, used their new military forces to pacify them was an augmentation of the influence of the rural nonofficial gentry within their provinces.

Increased Provincial Power

The appointment of the organizers of the Hunan and Huai armies to high provincial posts marked a breach in the elaborate system of checks and balances by means of which the dynasty had intended to forestall any challenge to its rule. Separation of civil and military authority into two parallel bureaucracies each dependent upon the court and the central government had been a keystone of that policy. Three large consequences were associated with the concession to realpolitik which the suppression of the mid-century rebellions forced Peking to accept: a diminution of central control over appointment to provincial and local office, the perpetuation of formidable armed forces not under the full control of the Board of War in the capital, and a decrease in the central government's command over the fiscal resources of the provinces. To what extent was the center weakened and the power of the provinces (or "regions" in some instances, if one bears in mind the dominance of Tseng Kuo-fan and Li Hung-chang over all of the Yangtze provinces from Wuhan to Shanghai during the 1860s, or Li's paramount position in North China for the quarter-century before 1895) enhanced?

It is not unlikely that men of the calibre of Tseng and Li (chin-shih, Han-lin experience, good connections) would have risen to high office even without the Taiping and Nien rebellions. The fact is, however, that it was their leadership of effective "personal" armies against the rebels which brought them their formal provincial appointments. Other post-Taiping governors-general and governors--Tso Tsung-t'ang, Liu Ming-ch'uan, Shen Pao-chen, Li Han-chang, and Liu K'un-i are examples--also first came into prominence as military leaders. From the 1860s the selection of the second echelon of provincial officials--the financial and judicial commisssioners who had earlier been considered as agents of the capital bureaucracy --was strongly influenced by the governors-general and governors. These men, moreover, were usually able to have their personal choices appointed to particularly critical local posts, for example as military administrative taotai (ping-pei tao) in the treaty port areas. And the creation of new positions outside of the regular territorial hierarchy (superintendents of customs, officers in the new armies, managers of modern arsenals and other "self-strengthening" enterprises, and likin supervisors) provided opportunities for the placement of yet other followers. The unusually long tenures in one post of such governors-general as Li Hung-chang (Chihli, 1870-1895), Liu K'un-i (Liang-Chiang, 1879-1881, 1891-1902), and Chang Chih-tung (Hu-Kuang, 1889-1907), moveover, was a departure from the Ch'ing practice of rotating officials from post to post so as to prevent the accretion of local ties that might abridge the central government's influence over its top provincial appointees.

For the governors-general and governors and all their subordinate civil and military officials remained de jure the appointees of the center; the court never relinquished its fundamental power to appoint and dismiss. Even if often in practice Peking was limited to ratifying rather than initiating the selection of part of the provincial bureaucracy, this too was a real power. A governor-general or governor who was concerned about his own career and standing in the bureaucracy did not lightly nominate candidates whom the court would not otherwise have accepted. The Board of Civil Service filled many lower provincial posts without reference to the governors; and in the post-Taiping decades large numbers (nearly half according to one analysis of the partial data available) of chou and hsien magistracies and some higher posts too, continued to be filled by men who had purchased official rank or title and/or the offices themselves, thus further reducing the scope of the local appointments which were controlled by the provincial leaders. Above all, the top provincial officials were genuinely loyal to the emperor, they normally accepted the decisions of Peking, and acknowledged in practice that they and their subordinates could be appointed, dismissed, transferred, and retired without any recourse when the court so ordered.

Apart from the diminution in the importance of the provincial treasurer who had been the Board of Revenue's man in the provincial administration and the accompanying decline in Peking's information about provincial tax receipts and disbursements, the growth of the locally controlled likin revenue was the most important mid-century change in the fiscal relations between center and province. A tax on goods in transit which was sometimes collected as well at the point of destination, likin is said to have been first introduced in 1853 in Kiangsu province; it was adopted as a measure to finance the anti-Taiping war in Hunan, Hupei, and Kiangsi in 1855, and soon was levied in all the provinces of the empire. In the period before the Taipings and Nien were suppressed, the central government was rarely even informed about the size of provincial likin receipts; thus, without being able to give any accurate figure, one can only say that it provided a third of the funds expended by the Hunan and Huai armies. After the end of the rebellions, although the provincial authorities were required to report their likin receipts annually to the Board of Revenue, only about twenty per cent of the reported amount (for example, Tls. 15 million reported in 1868, Tls. 14 million in the 1890s) was disposed of by the central government, the balance remaining under the de facto control of the provinces. And the unreported collection, of unknown size but said to be equal to the known collection, of course was also retained locally. Balancing the accretion to provincial fiscal independence which came with this large new revenue are the facts that the newly instituted Imperial Maritime Customs after 1854 regularized the collection of duties on foreign trade and channelled these growing receipts (Tls. 6 million annually in the 1860s, Tls. 22 million in 1893) to the Peking government rather than to the provinces; the land tax and grain tribute quotas due to Peking annually were regularly remitted by the provinces; and when it was urgently demanded, though he might procrastinate, no governor-general or governor could risk totally denying the central government's demands for large remittances from likin to meet emergencies.

Unlike the Banners and the Green Standard battalions which went into a final decay after the 1860s, the regional armies of Tseng Kuo-fan and Li Hung-chang, and of other provincial leaders like Tso Tsung-t'ang, Liu K'un-i, and Chang Chih-tung who followed their lead in organizing yung forces, were not subject to direct central control. Efforts to construct a modern centralized army came only after the

humiliation of defeat by Japan in 1894-1895, and had serious unantic-
ipated consequences. The post-Taiping situation represented a major
departure from the Ch'ing dynasty's fundamental policy of maintaining
the court's command over all the armed forces in the empire and
deploying these troops in such a fashion that they could not be easily
concentrated to threaten its rule. From early in the dynasty the
widely dispersed Chinese Green Standard units had been counterbalanced
by larger strategically located Banner encampments. Now neither was
any longer an effective fighting force, and the best troops in the empire were "personal" armies commanded by Chinese provincial leaders.
Yet there was not the least inclination on the part of these commanders to employ their armies against the Manchu dynasty. Tseng and
the others accepted the necessity and correctness of seeking imperial
approval of their military actions; the court's influence on the diversion of funds from the provinces to support, for example, Tso Tsung-
t'ang in the northwest or Li Hung-chang's Huai Army in north China
remained important; the officers of the new regional armies took
seriously the military ranks and titles for which they were beholden
to the Board of War. Whatever the situation had been in the seventeenth century immediately after the Manchu conquest, in the mid-
nineteenth century no important Chinese official yet harbored anti-
Manchu designs. The new armies and the modest armaments industry
which was initiated in the 1860s and then gradually expanded, in fact,
were primarily directed to the suppression of internal disorder which
might threaten the dynasty. They may not have been very effective
against the foreigner, but they were adequate to subdue the local
secret society uprisings, the endemic banditry, and the antimission-
ary riots which occurred at frequent intervals in the last half of the
century. Note that there were no further major rebellions, with the
exception of the rather special case of the Boxers, before the dynasty
fell in 1911.

I conclude as follows from this rehearsal of the pros and cons
of the argument that the progressive weakening of the Ch'ing central
government was a major consequence of the rebellions of the nineteenth century: Indeed, as compared with the decades of Ch'ien-lung's
glorious rule, a devolution of central power had occurred. But it was
only a partial devolution, and it is difficult to see a simple monocausal
chain from the enhancement of provincial authority just described to
the collapse of the dynasty in 1911. The incapacity of the state undoubtedly retarded "modernization," and undercut China's ability to
repel foreign imperialism, but the dynasty and imperial state did not
simply wither away. They expired because even the rural gentry,

whose local power was refurbished and probably augmented after the
suppression of the rebellions, came to expect too much of them; and
because other members of the same elite, who had left the countryside for the city and had been gradually exposed to foreign ideas and
manners, were prepared to attempt to organize a polity which was
not founded upon a commitment to imperial Confucianism.

Strengthening of the Local Gentry

Pacification of rebellion by Tseng, Li, Tso and their subordinates involved not only military victory but also restoration of normal civil government and reestablishment of local control The great
rebellions had resulted in enormous physical destruction, disruption
of the examination system in rebel held areas, breakdown of local
police and fiscal institutions, and a palpable decline in popular mo-
rale. By both tangible and intangible means the new provincial leader
sought to remedy these ills. The key to recovery was the Confucian
gentry who nurtured the officials of the imperial bureaucracy and provided the backbone of the rural social order.

Tseng Kuo-fan's program in areas that he recovered from the
Taipings included the immediate reinstatement of the civil service
examinations. Two months after the recovery of Nanking he requested
the despatch of officials from Peking to conduct the winter provincial
examination. Similarly Tso Tsung-t'ang in Shensi announced the holding of the long overdue examinations as soon as he had pacified that
province. Moreover, the statutory quotas for chü-jen and especially
sheng-yuan degrees were increased in many localities after 1864.
While the critical chin-shih quota was not augmented and the chü-jen
increase was slight, so that entrance into the higher bureaucracy was
not eased, the probable twenty per cent growth in the number of
sheng-yuan during the last half of the century did enhance the status
of the nonofficial elite as a group in their localities. It might be
noted that in the middle decades of the century there was widespread
opposition to suggestions that the content of the examinations be
changed to include modern subjects. The gentry were further pa-
tronized by substantial efforts to revive Confucian scholarship and
learning, which carried the implicit and traditional assumption that
if the gentry's belief in the Confucian teaching were deepened the
peasantry too would be indoctrinated by that example. Thus schools
and academies which had suffered during the rebellions were rebuilt
and their endowment lands restored to them, efforts were made to

recover and rehouse the scattered books from the great private libraries in Kiangsu and Chekiang which the Taipings had destroyed, and new editions of the Classics and Histories were printed under the auspices of Tseng Kuo-fan in Kiangnan and Tso Tsung-t'ang in the northwest. And to strengthen the gentry self-image, and thus the their status and loyalty, such eulogistic publications as the Chung-lieh pei-k'ao [Record of gentry martyrs; 1876] were issued.

To restore the traditional economy in the areas where civil war had wrought great destruction, pre-Taiping land titles were confirmed, land tax reductions were initiated especially in the lower Yangtze provinces, and official help was given to reclaim the agricultural land which had been abandoned. All of these measures benefitted the local elite much more than they did the populace as a whole. Though Feng Kuei-fen (1809-1874), who was the major proponent of tax relief, couched his recommendations in terms of uniformly reducing rates in the interest of all, gentry and commoners, in practice the greater influence of the wealthier families and their actual involvement in the collection process guaranteed that tax relief was an important material gesture in favor of the local leaders of the gentry resistance to the rebellions. In any case, by the mid-1870s the miscellaneous surcharges which had been temporarily curbed in Kiangsi, Kiangsu, Chekiang, Anhwei, Hunan, and Hupei were being restored. Abandoned lands were sold preferentially to those who had the funds to pay cash; litigation over title to disputed lands tended to favor the more influential gentry; and some purchased land was acquired by new owners in fee simple, i.e., was let to tenants without the right of perpetual cultivation (yung-t'ien) which had been fairly widespread in the lower Yangtze area and moderated somewhat the hardships of tenancy. And, of course, no one yet seriously advocated a reduction of tenant rents.

The growth of likin into an important local and provincial revenue source, although it did not replace the tax on land which remained the single largest levy at the disposal of Peking, probably reduced the potential fiscal pressure on agriculture in the decades before the end of the century, and this indirectly benefitted (although not in equal degrees) both the landowning gentry and the peasant proprietor. And given the regressive nature of the other levies--in addition to likin and duties on foreign trade whose collections increased after mid-century--such as the tax on salt and miscellaneous consumption taxes, the rural gentry were, relatively speaking, also beneficiaries.

Although the evidence on this matter is still scanty, I believe that it will show that there was a tendency for the local gentry to play a more formal role in subdistrict government in the post-Taiping decades. The gentry's critical and dominant place in rural society we have noted several times, but by both gentry preference and imperial design it had been sanctioned not so much by formal leadership of state-established institutions as by their higher economic, educational, cultural, and legal status. In the Ch'ing pao-chia (surveillance and registration) system, for example, the pao and chia headmen were by regulation commoners and not members of the gentry. Pao-chia was an imperial effort to superimpose a state-organized institution on the "natural" units of rural society in the interest of social control. As the gentry were the leaders of village society, in order to subject them as well as the peasantry to control the pao-chia officers were selected from outside of their ranks. Pao-chia, if it had ever really worked except for population registration, was a shambles in mid-century, both cause and effect of the phenomena of social disorder that I have analyzed in this chapter. Part of the effort by Tseng Kuo-fan and others to restore civil government and social order called for the revival of pao-chia, which took the form in many localities of gentry leaders formally assuming the duties of pao-chia headmen.

A similar process took place in the li-chia tax collection system. This, like pao-chia, was also an imperial effort to insert a state-organized institution into local society below the level of the hsien. To expect the commoner li-chia headmen to be able to withstand either the extortions of yamen runners and petty clerks or the tax evasions of the local gentry was even more unrealistic than the hope that the powerless pao-chia leaders would be able to control crime. By the mid-nineteenth century it was already fairly common though illegal for wealthy gentry families (referred to as ta-hu, big householders, in contrast to hsiao-hu, small or commoner households) to collect and pay the land tax on behalf of small peasant proprietors. The process provided income for the gentry who were subject to lighter surcharges by the official collectors than were commoners, and some benefit to the peasant clients with whom the gentry split the difference. When gentry associations in the last half of the century in a number of instances formally assumed a place in the hierarchy of tax collection units, it was first as a means of providing regular funding for antirebel militia units. After the suppression of the rebellions, top provincial officials at least condoned the extension of this process as a means of curbing the excesses of subofficial yamen underlings who, proverbially at least, benefitted the most from the land tax.

The new likin collectorates too became a special preserve of the local elite, and a major source of the financing for the gentry-led militia and the regional armies which grew out of them. At the numerous small branch stations, official supervision was difficult; even after the rebellions were over funds were diverted to the interest of local gentry-sponsored projects or to their purses. A web of vested interests grew up linked by personal ties which the high provincial officials had difficulty in dominating. Likin was not abolished until 1931 in spite of much agitation and many negotiations; the opposition to curbing it came not just from high officials, but also from that part of the gentry which had retained its rural character.

There is at least one major issue clouding this picture of restored and augmented gentry power in rural China after the suppression of the mid-century rebellions. How are we to evaluate the continuing and probably even increasing sale of chien-sheng (student of the Imperial College) academic titles in the last half of the century? The title brought gentry privileges, but it did not necessarily mean that the purchaser was well-trained in Confucian learning. Did it not therefore also dilute--at least in their own eyes and possibly to all traditional beholders--the quality and value of being a member of the local elite? If we guess that most chien-sheng, even at mid-century and increasingly so in later decades, were not located at the lower ranges of rural society, but were urban merchants, compradors, small entrepreneurs and managers, military men, or one of the growing number of regular gentry sons who had left the village for the treaty ports or other cities--then the cloud overhead mostly disappears and we are simultaneously introduced to a social stratum which figures importantly in the history of last decades of the Ch'ing dynasty. For the most part, however, the refurbished local society and the strengthened elite within it remained traditional in their outlook, so much so that they would both impede domestic change and reject the foreign presence.

SUGGESTIONS FOR FURTHER READING

Chiang, Siang-tseh. The Nien Rebellion. Seattle: University of Washington Press, 1954.

Chu, Wen-chang. The Moslim Rebellion in Northwest China, 1862-1878. The Hague: Mouton, 1966.

Freedman, Maurice. Chinese Lineage and Society: Fukien and Kwangtung. London: Athlone Press, 1966.

_____. Lineage Organization in Southeastern China. London: Athlone Press, 1958.

Jen, Yu-wen (Chien, Yu-wen). The Taiping Revolutionary Movement. New Haven: Yale University Press, 1973.

Kuhn, Philip A. Rebellion and Its Enemies in Late Imperial China: Militarization and Social Structure, 1796-1864. Cambridge: Harvard University Press, 1970.

Michael, Franz H. The Taiping Rebellion: History and Documents, 3 vols. Seattle: University of Washington Press, 1966-71.

Shih, Vincent Y. C. The Taiping Ideology: Its Sources, Interpretations, and Influences. Seattle: University of Washington Press, 1967.

Spector, Stanley. Li Hung-chang and the Huai Army: A Study in Nineteenth-Century Chinese Regionalism. Seattle: University of Washington Press, 1964.

Teng, Ssü-yü. The Nien Army and Their Guerrilla Warfare. Paris: Mouton, 1961.

_____. The Taiping Rebellion and the Western Powers: A Comprehensive Survey. Oxford: Clarendon Press, 1971.

Yang, Ch'ing-k'un. Religion in Chinese Society. Berkeley: University of California Press, 1961.

MICHIGAN PAPERS IN CHINESE STUDIES

No. 1. The Chinese Economy, 1912-1949, by Albert Feuerwerker.

No. 2. The Cultural Revolution: 1967 in Review, four essays by Michel Oksenberg, Carl Riskin, Robert Scalapino, and Ezra Vogel.

No. 3. Two Studies in Chinese Literature: "One Aspect of Form in the Arias of Yüan Opera" by Dale Johnson; and "Hsü K'o's Huang Shan Travel Diaries" translated by Li Chi, with an introduction, commentary, notes, and bibliography by Chun-shu Chang.

No. 4. Early Communist China: Two Studies: "The Fu-t'ien Incident" by Ronald Suleski; and "Agrarian Reform in Kwangtung, 1950-1953" by Daniel Bays.

No. 5. The Chinese Economy, ca. 1870-1911, by Albert Feuerwerker.

No. 6. Chinese Paintings in Chinese Publications, 1956-1968: An Annotated Bibliography and An Index to the Paintings, by E. J. Laing.

No. 7. The Treaty Ports and China's Modernization: What Went Wrong? by Rhoads Murphey.

No. 8. Two Twelfth Century Texts on Chinese Painting, "Shan-shui ch'un-ch'üan chi" by Han Cho, and chapters nine and ten of "Hua-chi" by Teng Ch'un, translated by Robert J. Maeda.

No. 9. The Economy of Communist China, 1949-1969, by Chu-yuan Cheng.

No. 10. Educated Youth and the Cultural Revolution in China by Martin Singer.

No. 11. Premodern China: A Bibliographical Introduction, by Chun-shu Chang.

No. 12. Two Studies on Ming History, by Charles O. Hucker.

No. 13. Nineteenth Century China: Five Imperialist Perspectives, selected by Dilip Basu, edited with an introduction by Rhoads Murphey.

No. 14. Modern China, 1840-1972: An Introduction to Sources and Research Aids, by Andrew J. Nathan.

No. 15. Women in China: Studies in Social Change and Feminism, edited with an introduction by Marilyn B. Young.

No. 16. An Annotated Bibliography of Chinese Painting Catalogues and Related Texts, by Hin-cheung Lovell.

No. 17. China's Allocation of Fixed Capital Investment, 1952-57, by Chu-yuan Cheng.

No. 18. Health, Conflict, and the Chinese Political System, by David M. Lampton.

No. 19. Chinese and Japanese Music-Dramas, edited by J. I. Crump and William P. Malm.

No. 20. Hsin-lun (New Treatise) and Other Writings by Huan T'an (43 B.C.-28 A.D.), translated by Timoteus Pokora.

No. 21. Rebellion in Nineteenth-Century China, by Albert Feuerwerk

Price: $3.00 (US) each
except $4.00 for special issues #6, #15, and #19
and $5.00 for special issue #20

Prepaid Orders Only

NON SERIES PUBLICATION

Index to the "Chan-Kuo Ts'e", by Sharon Fidler and J. I. Crump.
A companion volume to the Chan-Kuo Ts'e translated by J. I. Crump
(Oxford: Clarendon Press, 1970). $3.00

MICHIGAN ABSTRACTS OF CHINESE AND
JAPANESE WORKS ON CHINESE HISTORY

No. 1. The Ming Tribute Grain System by Hoshi Ayao, translated
by Mark Elvin.

No. 2. Commerce and Society in Sung China by Shiba Yoshinobu,
translated by Mark Elvin.

No. 3. Transport in Transition: The Evolution of Traditional
Shipping in China, translations by Andrew Watson.

No. 4. Japanese Perspectives on China's Early Modernization: The
Self-Strengthening Movement, 1860-1895 by K. H. Kim.

Price: $4.00 (US) each

Prepaid Orders Only

Michigan Papers and Abstracts available from:
Center for Chinese Studies
University of Michigan
Lane Hall
Ann Arbor, Michigan 48104
USA